Hollyhock Days

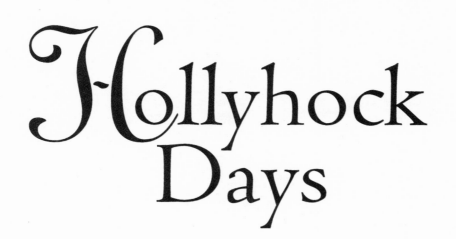

Hollyhock Days

Garden Adventures for the Young at Heart

WRITTEN & ILLUSTRATED

BY SHARON LOVEJOY

INTERWEAVE PRESS

 INTERWEAVE PRESS, INC.
201 East Fourth Street
Loveland, Colorado 80537

Cover and interior design: Susan Wasinger, Signorella Graphic Arts
Editorial Consultant: Mary Ann Telatnik
Production: Marc McCoy Owens

Library of Congress Cataloging-in-Publication Data

Lovejoy, Sharon, 1945–
    Hollyhock days : garden adventures for the young at heart / Sharon Lovejoy.
       p.   cm.
    Includes bibliographical references (p. 92).
    ISBN 1-883010-01-2 : $24.95. — ISBN 0-934026-90-4 : $16.95
    1. Gardening.   2. Nature craft.   I. Title.
SB455.L66   1994
635--dc20
                                    94-19071
                                     CIP

First printing: 10M:994:ARC:Ppb
              7M:994:ARC:Hdb
Second printing: 7.5M:495:QUE:Ppb

Dedication

To Noah, who always believed in me.
To Jeff, who taught me to believe in myself.

Special thanks to my dearest friend Julie Whitmore for her unfailing support and inspiration. To Susan Wasinger of Signorella Graphic Arts for her fine and sensitive book design. To Linda Ligon for her patience, quiet sense of humor, and integrity. All of the great staff at Interweave Press, especially Karen Evanson, Karen Gogela, and Gail Jones. And to Mary Harris, my favorite advocate.

All of the ladies at my shop, Heart's Ease—Roberta Baker, Victoria Greene, Anabel Royer, Dianna Freeman, Monica Zuvic, Jennifer Molinari, Anna Molinari, my eccentric winter employee from Maine, Marilyn Brewer. Teresa Lees, Michael Freeman, and my dear friend Patrick Gannon, the shop dad. I could never accomplish anything without your combined energy, creativity, and support.

Foreword

If a memory can influence the future, the one I have of meeting Sharon Lovejoy several years ago while on a trip to photograph her remarkable home and garden, Seekhaven, does just that. Immediately, her depth of knowledge and her intense love of all manner of plants and animals struck a deep chord; we commenced a friendship which has flourished across the many miles and months that have separated us since.

From her burgeoning community garden and shop, Heart's Ease, in tiny, charming Cambria, California, Sharon conducts similar correspondences with acquaintances around the globe. The richness of Sharon's vision first epitomized in *Sunflower Houses,* the sister volume to *Hollyhock Days,* engendered a new passion and respect for nature among young and old.

Gardener, poet, naturalist, teacher, artist, ambassador of the joys of the garden, Sharon celebrates the beauty of childhood memories, rainbow colors, and sun-warmed fragrances. She proves that all that is ephemeral is perhaps all that lasts. Above all, *Hollyhock Days* teaches that it is never too late to begin a tradition, to develop a bond, to enhance our lives. Why not begin with this delightful tome, and then, on to the garden. . . .

Niña Williams, Editor
Country Living Gardener

Preface

THE MOST EFFECTIVE KIND OF EDUCATION IS THAT

A CHILD SHOULD PLAY

AMONGST LOVELY THINGS.

—PLATO

Dear gardening friend,

My tiny workroom is filled with the flickering sunlight shining through the needles of the shaggy-barked cedar. A rainbow-hued company of hollyhocks sway and scratch their backs on the old stone wall. In the distance, I can hear the wavering call of the quail and the mingled laughter of acorn woodpeckers and playing children. The sounds and dappled light tell me, without aid of a calendar, that it is summer—glorious, fragrant, rustling summer—hollyhock days. Time for gardens and time for me to sit down and get busy.

Since writing my last book, *Sunflower Houses,* I've been in touch with wonderful people from all over the world. Every day the mailbox holds the promise of new friends and constant surprises. It now is a ritual to pick up my mail, brew a pot of ginger tea in my Nonie's old teapot, and settle down on the willow chair to read, surrounded by a romping pumpkin vine that threatens to engulf me and my stand of red sunflowers. Many of the letters I've received have asked me for another book.

And so, my gardening friends, let me offer you some more quiet moments of discovery. *Hollyhock Days* is a sister volume to *Sunflower Houses*, a colorful album of gardening legend, lore, and fact sewn and sown together with the memories, ideas, dreams, and creativity of hundreds of people.

Please remember to share with children the simple gift of time in a garden. The time you share with them will also remind you that it is never too late, as Richard Henry Dana wrote in the 1840s, to "In heart be a child."

Sharon Lovejoy
CAMBRIA PINES-BY-THE-SEA

Acknowledgments

To my newly discovered friend Skippy Shoemaker, the original sunflower house creator, and to her daughter Ginny Kirschenman for sharing the story and uniting us. The Hogue family, Jane, Jack, Janna, Emily, and Tyler of the Prairie Pedlar, Odebolt, Iowa, for creating and maintaining the American family dream and providing constant inspiration. Maria Grimaldi at Catskill Morning Herb Farm in Youngsville, New York. Artist Laurie Archer of Santa Fe, New Mexico, for her hollyhock memories. Houston Knight, the gentleman with the mulberry hide-out. Michael Emmons of Laughing Willows. Eugene Kociba, horticulturist at Fernwood Botanic Gardens in Niles, Michigan. Diana Van de Kamp for informing me that "the very best carrots are the warped ones." The irrepressible Dr. Arthur O. Tucker, Delaware State College. Heidi Hughes, American Bat Conservation Society, for caring and sharing. Susan Strahan, Itasca, Texas, for sending me the wonderful quote from Plato. Betty Cerar, "young carrots in love" lady from Palgrave, Ontario, Canada. My friend Gerry Bullington Bauman, The Herb Farm, Grimes, Iowa. My pal Jane Dicus in Winston-Salem, North Carolina, for searching out great poems and treasures.

C O N T E N T S

C O N T E N T S

Plans and Dreams and Garden Schemes

CHAPTER ONE

LONG, STRAIGHT ROWS

ARE SUCH A BORE!

GARDENS SHOULDN'T

BE A CHORE!

ou don't need fancy tools and a big yard to be a gardener. In fact, some of my best gardens have been in pots, tubs, and boxes. My favorite garden tool has always been a big kitchen spoon I borrowed from my mom. You *do* need a sense of humor, good ideas, good soil, water, sunshine, and seeds or plant starts. And, of course, worms!

I learned how to garden as a child working by my Grandmother Lovejoy's side. I got to know the names of plants, birds, butterflies, and bugs just by being outside with them, watching them, listening to them. They were my constant companions, they became my friends. And as my own son grew, I shared my friends and special memories with him.

Some days, I just stretched out on the hillside and spent hours popping open the thick door of the trapdoor spider's home. I liked watching the fat spider run up her hallway and close the door. Other days I helped Grandmother plant bulbs and seeds or "uncrowd" the iris.

When I helped Grandmother weed (we had contests to see who could weed the fastest), I couldn't help picking up seeds, too. I had a basket of little envelopes. When I found a prize flower that had gone to seed, I would tape one of the seeds to the outside of the envelope, write the name of the plant and the date I collected it, and carefully put the rest of the seeds inside it. I kept all of those envelopes in a dark, dry drawer. Then, the next spring, Grandmother would help me plant all those seeds outside. We had pretty good luck, too.

Grandmother and I had certain jobs that we tended to daily. Watering during dry weather was a must, and very time-consuming. We always watered early in the morning to help the plants make it through the long, hot day. She showed me how to take my time and give the plants a long, deep, gentle drink, and how to stick my finger in the soil afterward to make sure it was really wet deep down. Some people like to water at night, but we would talk about how hard it would be to be thirsty and dry all day long without any drink until evening. Grandmother helped me learn to look at plants and figure out how I would like to be treated if I were a plant.

There were never any hard and fast rules in our garden, except to be kind to the plants and animals, clean up after ourselves, and never, ever say "dirt". *Soil* is what plants grow in, not dirt. Grandmother said that dirt is what gets under your fingernails.

Every single day I watched as Grandmother scrubbed the hummingbird feeder that hung from a bottlebrush tree right outside our kitchen window. She taught me that the feeder must be clean or the hummingbirds would get sick and die.

One of my jobs was to make sure that the birdbaths (we had three) were filled at least once a day. I learned that the birds always need fresh water, even in the middle of winter. Sometimes, as

THE RAINBOW

I know a blue hill

Not so very high,

Where the rainbow ribbons

Are thrown across the sky

Some day and some day,

After a shower,

I shall climb the hill and be

Back in half an hour.

I shall wind the rainbow

Upon an empty spool

And put it in my pocket

Where it is dark and cool.

I shall pick a yellow star

And I shall pick another,

And hide them in my apron

To carry home to Mother

From
AFTER THE RAIN
by Grace Hallock

The Flower Girl

I'm going to the garden
Where summer roses blow
I'll make me a little sister
Of all the flowers that grow.

I'll make her body of lilies
Because they're soft and white
I'll make her eyes of violets
With dew drops shining bright
I'll make her lips of rose-buds
Her cheeks of rose leaves red
Her hair of silky corn tops
All braided round her head.

With apple tree and pear leaves
I'll make her a lovely gown
With rows of golden buttercups
for buttons up and down.
I'll dance with my little sister
Away to the river strand
Away across the water
Away into fairy land.

CHARLES G. LELAND

I filled the shallow saucers with a fine spray of water, a hummingbird would fly right down and take a bath! I felt as if someone had given me a special gift.

All year long we fed the birds. We had trays of seed for the morning doves, towhees, and jays; we had socks of suet for the chickadees and nuthatches, and a ground feeding area for the tame flocks of quail that came down from the hills. Not all birds like to eat the same things at the same kind of feeder. Some like to eat up high on a flat area, others love to hang, still others, like orioles and hummingbirds, love to sip nectar.

Grandmother taught me so much as we worked out in the garden. I learned that worms love birthday cake, that snails love beer (their bad habit is their undoing), that most snakes are garden helpers, that some plants are poison, that lilac blossoms slip neatly inside each other to make a perfect necklace, that willows can be called *willgrows* because they "will grow" wherever you plant them.

Put Out a Welcome Mat

A boy once wrote and asked me if it was okay to save a spot

"for the wild things." Of course it is! Leave a corner or a border natural and you will be surprised at all of the visitors you will have. Many birds, butterflies, and other critters depend on "wild" spots to survive. Your garden can be a haven for everything from the tiniest ladybug to a friendly gopher snake. You might see a blazing goldfinch hanging upside down, picking seeds from a thistle. Soon you'll recognize him, not just by sight, but by his song. He will become an old friend.

A LETTER FROM MY FRIENDS JACK AND JANE HOGUE

Jack and I have gathered everlasting memories by including our children in the garden venture. Conversation among the rows of delphinium and yarrow reveal many tender secrets. Daughters share friends' dilemmas, heartaches of youth, and anxious moments from school. Son speaks of playground triumphs and future dreams. As parents, we listen intently to their woes, offer gentle words, and nurture their young ambitions. Gardening together, our children have grown deep, not just tall. Our family roots are sturdy and secure. The children have found perennial love at home—in the gardens. When they glance back at their childhood, they, too, will remember that they grew best in the sunshine among the flowers.

Plant your seeds in a row,
•
One for the pheasant,
•
One for the crow,
•
One to rot
•
and one to grow!

—Old Song

You will see beautiful butterflies. Some will be dancing quietly from weed to weed, sipping at their favorite blossoms. Others will be laying eggs in a sheltered spot either on or close to a favored food plant. When the eggs hatch, you can almost hear the young caterpillars chomping.

You may stumble across a plump, baggy, grouchy-looking toad. He loves sheltered wild areas and will rest there during the day. In the evening he will slowly patrol your garden and gobble up the pesky bugs eating your favorite melon vine.

A wild garden will always give you something new to learn.

You can start a garden at any age. When the children are grown; when you want to spend time with grandchildren, nieces and nephews, godchildren, or with the only child in the neighborhood who has no one to play with. When you are no longer tied to a 9-to-5 job, or when you take two weeks off just for you. A garden can be your favorite place, a secret place—maybe only big enough for you and the fairies or a toad.

A LITTLE RAIN AND A LITTLE SUN—
AND A LITTLE PEARLY DEW—
AND A PUSHING UP
AND A REACHING OUT
THEN, LEAVES AND TENDRILS ALL ABOUT!
—FROM AN OLD SONG

Compost

There are whole books on the right way to make compost. You can buy plastic bins, or wire ones. You can, as one gentleman does, put garden and kitchen waste in an old clothes dryer. You can have a regular schedule for turning it upside down, add special chemicals, take its temperature. Or you can just build a simple "possibilities" pile.

When you throw out leftovers—rice, bread, cabbage, carrots, cereal, potatoes—you are throwing away possibilities. Possibilities for beautiful fruits and flowers, plump red earthworms, and lots of healthy birds and other valuable critters in your garden. Dead leaves, plant thinnings, lawn clippings, pine needles—these are "possibilities", too.

My grandparents always had a compost pile. They never did a thing to it except add table scraps and lawn clippings. It got watered when the lawn sprinklers came on. They never turned their compost heap, they just shoveled into the bottom of the pile whenever they needed humus and mulch for their prize-winning roses. That was one easy compost pile. They added to it and took from it for 67 years!

When you've been adding possibilities to your compost pile for a while, get brave and stick your hand deep into the middle. It should feel hot, which shows that you have healthy compost. It's breaking down, making good, rich, dark humus. Nothing fancy going on here, just nature!

THINGS YOU CAN DO TO HELP
YOUR COMPOST

*Put in a layer of grass clippings
or hedge trimmings*

—

Add a layer of vegetable left overs

—

Scoop in a layer of soil

—

Add available manure

—

Water your compost pile

*From time to time you can poke a shovel
or fork into your pile and turn it over.
Turning it helps to get air into the pile so
that the bacteria and fungi at work can
get enough oxygen to keep going.*

If earthworms could smile,

I'm sure you would see,

You make your worms happy

With kitchen debris.

But then, who can say,

If they smile or they frown,

The worm's little mouth

Always faces the GROUND!

The Girls

Another kind of possibilities pile I keep is the one that houses my "girls", my faithful, hungry, red earthworms. There are no better helpers in the garden! They quietly gnaw their way through all the goodies I give them, which turn into fabulous "black gold" (called "doo-good" by certain children I know).

When we had a horrible storm recently, trees blew down and knocked out our electricity. We went for three days without light or heat. Of course, everything in the freezer thawed out. What a feast for the girls! Eleven loaves of bread, rosemary and olive rolls, a cake (I think it was the fruitcake gift), frozen rice casserole—the mound was enormous! Think of it: eight years of forgotten food finally cleared out and hauled in loads to my worm bin.

I thought it would take a year for them to work their way through this accumulation, but it only took eleven days. Now I have the fattest red worms, the best pile of soil, and a clean refrigerator.

If you live in a city and don't have a place outdoors to keep a worm bin, you may have room under the kitchen sink for a small bucket. These girls are no trouble to keep indoors, and you never have to worry about them scratching to go out for a late-night walk. You can keep a big trash can of girls on a back porch or in the basement, too. Do *not* keep them outside where they might freeze, and do *not* put them in full sun where they will cook!

My friend Maria Grimaldi at Catskill Morning Herb Farm in Youngsville, New York, knows everything there is to know about gardens and soil. She keeps her girls indoors in a bucket with a thin layer of shavings in the bottom. Some people put in a few inches of gravel, then the shavings. Maria adds some leaves, grass, lettuce, or bread. She then drops in a handful of beautiful girls and sprinkles them a bit (not a lot—they can't swim). Finally, she covers the bucket with a lid. She keeps filling the bucket with goodies, and the girls keep eating, growing, casting garden gold, and making even more girls. They'll eat almost everything, but go lightly on citrus peels and coffee grounds.

Doo Panzda

Gifts from our Furry Friends

There are lots of other simple and natural ways to improve your garden. I have a young friend named Stephanie who has a wonderful fertilizer machine named Peter, a big, brown rabbit. Rabbits make clean, smart pets, and their droppings are great to add to your compost pile.

Rabbits aren't the only answer; chicken poop and goat doo work, too. An old friend of mine keeps horses. She makes a liquid fertilizer by dropping a horse apple or two in a bucket of water, and letting it sit for days until it looks like murky tea. Then she waters her plants with it. They love it, but once in a while she will get weed seeds sprouting in her plants. It's an amazing cycle: from seed to plant, plant to seeds, into the horse, through the horse, out of the horse, onto the ground, into her bucket, back into the ground, then more plants and more seeds.

My friend Maria Grimaldi mulches with thick, thick layers of newspaper. Maria and her friend Bella Stander laughed as they told me they always "mulch with the Times" (New York Times). It really does work! Soak the papers in a tub or bucket first and them spread on the ground. If you don't soak the papers first it is almost impossible to thoroughly wet them once they are in the ground. After you lay out a carpet of a few inches of newspaper, cut a hole where you want your plant to be. Plant your pumpkin or flower and then add a prettier layer of your real garden clipping mulch on top. Slowly but surely the newspaper and the mulch will break down. Your girls won't mind eating newspaper, they will be up on all the news!

Some people call seeds "treasure boxes" because they hold the treasure of life, food, health, and beauty. We see seeds every day without really seeing them: a roll covered with poppy seeds, a giant coconut, the false seeds on the outside of a stawberry.

Take a magnifying glass and really look at some seeds. Shell a fresh peanut and soak it in water overnight. The next day, cut it open and look at the cotyledon, or embryo—the undeveloped plant within the seed. Look at the small disc seeds of the hollyhock; they look like fairy money, papery thin and shiny.

What if every black seed on your poppy seed roll sprouted? What if every dandelion seed you ever wished on became a dandelion? What if every single pine cone that hit the earth and dropped out its cargo of seeds turned into a small forest of trees? Or how about all those maple seed helicopters you've seen twirling lazily down from the sky? There just isn't enough room on earth for every seed to grow.

Some seeds are transported and planted by wind (like the dandelion), some by water, birds, or animals. Flowers such as jewel weed, impatiens, wood sorrel, and violets have seed pods that suddenly explode, sending their seeds in every direction. Some lazy plants, like poppies and love-in-a-mist (nigella) simply open up their pods a bit and shake out their contents like salt from a shaker.

Take some time to put colored string and a

name tag on your favorite flowers. That way, after they've finished blooming and the seed heads have formed and dried, you can go back and find the ones you want and collect them in paper bags. Label the bags and put them away in a dark, dry closet. When they're completely dry, give the closed bags a few shakes and pour the seeds into small envelopes or other containers and label them.

I like to use the canisters that my camera film comes in. They are free and they keep seeds safe, dark, and dry. Put the seeds away, but don't put away your dreams and ideas for your next garden!

You can start growing new plants from seed before the snow has left the ground if you have a greenhouse, a cold frame, or just a warm, sunny windowsill. When my son Noah and I lived in a small cottage at the beach, we had every available windowsill crowded with pots, cups, crocks, and all sizes of jars jam-packed with plants we had started from seed. In our kitchen window we had a small apple orchard, all from seeds we had saved from lunch-box remains. On another windowsill stood a 10-inch tall grapefruit tree started from breakfast leftovers. We laughed about how funny it would look if our little windowsill tree were to bear a regular-size grapefruit.

> FIRST A SEED SO TINY, HIDDEN FROM THE SIGHT;
> THEN TWO PRETTY LEAFLETS STRUGGLING TOWARD THE LIGHT.
> —AN OLD SONG

Here is something to remember when you are sowing seeds. This isn't something you'll learn in school;

THE SMALLER SEEDS PLANT SHALLOW,

THE BIGGER SEEDS PLANT DEEPER,

IF YOU FORGET THESE SIMPLE RULES

YOUR SEEDS WILL ALL BE

S L E E P E R S !

Talking to Trees, Tickling Sunflowers

William Shakespeare once said,

"THERE ARE

tongues

IN TREES,

sermons

IN STONES, AND

books

IN RUNNING BROOKS."

You've seen a tree somehow growing in the crack of a sidewalk. Or a wildflower sprouting from a rock, or a fern growing in a crevice in a wall. How do they survive? The important thing is that they *do* survive, and sometimes are stronger for their hard times.

A few years ago I was working feverishly in my garden and noticed that my one and only lemon tree was in horrible condition. John Goetz was working on a terrace above me and he said, "That lemon tree is in such bad shape with scale and chlorosis and everything else; let's pull it out." I'm a softie and I was horrified.

For a while I just sat in the middle of a patch of oregano and thought about having to actually destroy a whole tree. I remembered a book I had read many years before that told how farmers would walk out into an orchard and give sickly trees a whack with a stick and a good talking to. Once a tree got a good scolding and a whack, it would often get better. I thought it was worth a try.

I waited until John left the garden, and then I grabbed the slender tree trunk and shook it. The whole time I was shaking it, I let it know in no uncertain terms that time was running out, that I'd give it only a couple more weeks, and then out of the ground and into the compost.

Every day I climbed the stone stairs to the upper herb garden and shook that lemon tree, all the while scolding it heartily. I have to admit, I did feel a little cruel; but someone had to do it.

After a week, I noticed that the infestation of scale had totally disappeared. I am not exaggerating. I did not treat it with any chemicals; they just plain disappeared. Slowly but surely, the health of the lemon tree changed. The leaves turned a rich, dark green, and shiny, waxy new buds appeared all over. Within weeks, the tree was starred with dozens of fragrant lemon blossoms and was the constant host of numerous quarrelsome hummingbirds.

A few years have passed. My lemon tree is twice as big as it was the day John delivered his ominous suggestion. It bears dozens of beautiful, juicy lemons each year. It makes the best lemonade, lemon pie, and pomanders. It has been a safe refuge for a family of towhees and a nest of hummingbirds. It constantly provides me with glorious, fragrant blooms and leaves for wreaths and bouquets and, better yet, the companionable hum of fuzzy-rumped bumblebees.

Since my lemon tree's close brush with death, I've always tried to spend a bit of extra time touching it and talking to it. You may think I'm crazy, but just recently I read that two Stanford University molecular biologists who were studying plant hormones found that spraying a certain hormone on a plant activated five genes. But these same five genes were activated when the plants were touched, or sprayed with a strong spray of water, or even blown with a hair dryer. The biologists noted that the plants that were touched, prodded, shaken, and squirted were much sturdier and stockier than the untouched plants. The untouched plants were taller, but weaker.

I always have believed that old wives' tales and folklore have their roots buried somewhere in the truth. And I'm always amazed at the mysteries and drama of life and death in the garden. There are so many unanswered questions! All you have to do is open your eyes and ears and remember to talk to your trees and tickle your sunflowers.

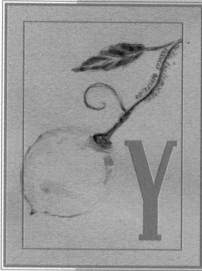

*Y*ou may hear the rustling of leaves and see the bursting bloom of the lilac and feel the warm earth . . . you are listening to the tongues in the trees, you are reading the messages from the earth. You are doing what the Native Americans did when they waited to plant until an oak leaf was as big as a squirrel's ear.

I've-Got-the-Blues Garden

Vita Sackville-West was one of the premier garden designers of the last century, taking great pleasure in planning and planting the gardens around Sissinghurst Castle in England. One of the most striking gardens at Sissinghurst is the white garden where all the flowering plants have white blooms. On the dark and dreary day I visited the castle, the garden shone brightly—each white face glowing through the veils of rain. It has been said that when color goes, fragrance comes, and that fragrance is the color of the night. Imagine wandering through that white garden, drenched in fragrance and alive with the whirring wings of nectar-feeding moths.

Although I love gardens that look like a crazy-quilt of every color in the rainbow, I also love gardens, like those at Sissinghurst, that devote themselves to one color. I got my inspiration for a blue garden from Vita Sackville-West and from an old book, *Keeper of the Bees*, by the naturalist Gene Stratton Porter:

> *He could see hollyhocks as high as the eaves of the house, and in many colours to the left and to the right he could sense the gay hues of nasturtiums and zinnias and marigolds, and his sensitive nostrils could pick up the tang of heliotrope, mignonette, and forget-me-nots and violets; but above everything else, he had the impression of a cloud of blue— sweet, restful blue. Facing the hives, around and near them, there was a world of blue: blue violets, heliotrope, forget-me-nots, blue verbenas, blue lilies, larkspur, bluebells, phlox, blue vervain, blue and yet more blue.*

Just close your eyes and picture all of those blues and the humming of the bees visiting each and every flower!

If you have room for a big bed of blue, or a small border

of blue, spend time walking through the rows of plants at the garden center and look for flowers that are really blue. Check out the seed racks, too. Tweedia, *Oxypetalum caeruleum*, is one of my favorite blues. This is a small shrub and does a bit of climbing in my garden. It has friendly, five-petaled, starry blue flowers that range from light blue when they are young to a dark blue as they age. This plant is tender and loves sun. With a bit of shade, it will freeze, so if you live in a cold area you will have to treat it as an annual.

I found another amazing blue while wandering through a long pergola at Reynolda Gardens in Winston-Salem, North Carolina. The pergola was totally covered with what I first thought were grapes, but soon learned were fascinating turquoise blue fruits smaller than marbles. The plant, commonly called turquoise vine, is *Ampelopsis brevipedunculata*. It produces berries of all of the variations of the color blue. They are incredibly beautiful and look wonderful in bouquets. If you have a sunny, warm wall or trellis near your blues garden you may be able to grow this successfully, especially if you live in the South or on the southern part of the West Coast. Easterners might be able to grow it during the summer in a sheltered spot, but it will need protection inside in the winter.

VIOLETS

If blue-birds bloomed like flowers in a row,
And never could make a sound,
How in the world would the violets know
When to come out of the ground?

—*From an 1800s song*

CHICORY
Cichoreum intybus

MORNING GLORY
Ipomoea purpurea
'HEAVENLY BLUE'

SQUILL
Scilla amoena

BOG SALVIA
Salvia uligosina

MONKSHOOD
Aconitum napellus

BABY BLUE EYES
Nemophila menziesii

NIGELLA
Nigella sativa

LOVE-IN-A-MIST
Nigella damascena

Dancing Through the Seasons

CHAPTER TWO

W HAT IS MORE GENTLE THAN A WIND

IN SUMMER?

WHAT IS MORE SOOTHING THAN THE

PRETTY HUMMER

THAT STAYS ONE MOMENT IN AN

OPEN FLOWER,

AND BUZZES CHEERILY FROM

BOWER TO BOWER?

– J O H N K E A T S , 1 8 1 6

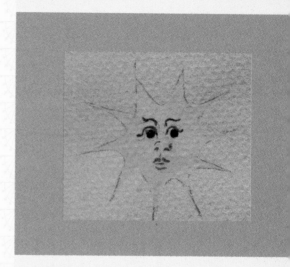

The Snow Moon

TIME TO PLOT
AND PLAN
AND DREAM
EACH AND EVERY GARDEN SCHEME.

In late January, start flower, herb, and vegetable seeds in peat pots or egg cartons and put them in a sunny, warm place. You'll have baby plants in a matter of days. Plant hollyhock seeds in peat pots to get an early start on your hollyhock tent.

To liven up the house during these dark days, cut branches of forsythia, plum, cherry, apple, and spirea and bring them inside. Put them in water and watch them come to life over the next few weeks. Experiment!

Save the wood ash from winter fires. Come summer you can add the ash to your soil. My roses love it. After spring rain showers, I put ashes around tender seedlings to ward off slugs.

*IF INTO COLD GROUND
goes the seed,
You'll harvest nothing
Except need.*

*"IF JANUARY 12TH IS CLEAR,
look for rain
all through the year."*

*IF THE OAK'S BEFORE THE ASH,
Then you'll only get a splash.
If the ash precedes the oak,
Then you'll surely get a soak.*

WHEN THE WIND IS IN THE EAST
'TIS GOOD FOR NEITHER
MAN,
NOR BEAST!

The Hunger Moon

ACORNS, SEEDS, AND BULBS ARE SET
UNDER EARTH'S THICK COVERLET.

Don't forget the birds! Make sure you provide a constant source of seed and water for them.

Go to a nursery. Spend time looking at the seed packets, the bare-root trees, and roses. See anything you love? Ask for a tree for Valentine's Day. It's better than candy in any number of ways.

If your birthday is on February 4th, your birthday flower is the pansy.

*I*n my gardens I always try to remember the birds with saucers of water and giant bouquets of wheat, corn, millet, and sorghum. I tie them to posts and bird feeders. They look beautiful in the bare winter garden, and they are a true treat for the birds.

THESE MOON NAMES TAKEN FROM "EVERYGIRLS: THE MAGAZINE OF THE CAMP FIRE GIRLS"

SEPTEMBER 1925

The Crow Moon

Sow sweet peas on St. Patrick's Day, March 17. It's one of those old wives' tales. I don't know why; just do it.

Here's a little French secret. Fill four 12-inch pots with rich soil. Mark seven evenly-spaced spots around the edge, and plant three sweet pea seeds in each spot. Stick a 6-foot bamboo stake in deeply near each group and one in the center; tie them together at the top. Keep the pots cool and well watered. By early summer you'll have a tepee of fragrant, colorful sweet peas.

WHEN APPLE BLOSSOMS
BLOOM AT NIGHT
FOR FIFTEEN DAYS,
NO RAIN IN SIGHT

Line a small basket with plastic wrap and fill it with soil. Plant the tiny plants the faeries love: primroses, pansies, thyme, maidenhair ferns, shamrocks, moss from the woods. Keep your faerie basket in a well-lit spot and water it only when it feels dry to the touch. If you turn on the light suddenly at night, you might catch fairy folk dancing.

April wet, ... *Good wheat.*

"APRIL SHOWERS BRING

MAY FLOWERS,"

OR SO THE SAYING GOES,

BUT I'M SPENDING HOURS,

WEEDING BETWEEN

SHOWERS,

SO MY FLOWERS HAVE

ROOM TO GROW!

APRIL:

The Wild Goose Moon

SKEINS OF GEESE HIGH OVERHEAD,
BURSTING BUD IN FLOWER BED.

Get a big half-barrel, fill it with loose, sandy soil with generous amounts of compost. *Don't* add the girls—they love potatoes. Plant seed potatoes—available from garden centers and catalogs—about 1 foot apart. Dress the soil with compost or hay or leaves on top. Put the barrel in full sun and give it plenty of water. You'll be able to start digging out tender little new potatoes by early summer.

Start marigolds, nasturtiums, and annual herbs indoors so they'll be ready to set out after all danger of frost is past.

Hollyhocks started in peat pots in January can now be transplanted into 4- to 6-inch pots.

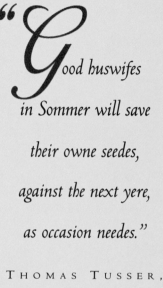

"*Good huswifes
in Sommer will save
their owne seedes,
against the next yere,
as occasion needes.*"

THOMAS TUSSER,
*Five Hundred Pointes of Good
Husbandrie,* 1573

To do my second through the air

all men have tried in vain,

And yet it may be often seen
Upon your window-pane.

My whole on summer nights is seen
A fairy lamp to light the green.

Answer to riddle: Fireflies.

Fireflies are actually flying beetles and their larvae eat slugs, snails and other insects.

MAY

The Song Moon

THE SONGS OF BIRDS WEND THROUGH THE TREES
AND LIFT AND LILT ON EVERY BREEZE.

Remember to read the directions on the backs of your seed packets. Better to plant too late than too early! Get those peat pots of seedlings ready to go outside as soon as the soil is warm. A nice thing about peat pots is that you can plant the whole thing, so touchy plants like morning glories and moon vines will be less disturbed.

The hollyhocks you started in November should be flourishing. Gently transplant them into the prepared soil in the trench outlining your hollyhock tent. Treat them to some of your "possibilities" compost and some worms.

JUNE

The Rose Moon

FULL-FACED ROSES NOD AND BOW
WE MUST GROOM AND TEND THEM NOW.

Herbs are steadfast, easy-going, easy-growing, forgiving, productive plants. You can use them for flavoring, craft projects, good smells, and just the sheer pleasure of kinship in the garden.

Choose rosemary. The name comes from *rosmarinus*, dew of the sea. Rosemary loves seaspray, but you can satisfy its need with your garden hose.

Try the "little dragon" plant, tarragon, too. This is one you can't grow from seed, so get a start from a friend or from your garden center.

The days are deliciously long now, with plenty of time to play and plant. You should get your gourds and squashes in early this month. If you want pumpkins by Halloween, you have to allow 90 to 115 days for them to mature.

The hollyhock is the birthday flower for June 25—lucky you!

JULY

The Thunder Moon

SOAK THE FEET AND SPARE THE HEAD,
OR YOUR FLOWERS WILL SOON BE DEAD.

Weed, weed, weed and don't forget to deadhead. This sinister-sounding activity, picking the spent blossoms off your flowering plants, keeps them from putting all their energy into making seeds, so they make more flowers instead. Let a few flowers go to seed, though, so that you'll have some to save for next year's garden. July, August, and September are seed-saving months.

When the fly's

———————

upon the wall

———————

Rain is surely

———————

going to fall

AUGUST:

The Green Corn Moon

WHO'LL BE TALLEST COME THE MORN?
THE LANKY RED HOLLYHOCK OR THE GREEN CORN?

Harvest your blooming lavender, and collect and dry other herbs for winter use. Gather your herbs early in the morning after the dew has dried. Bunch them together, tie with string, and hang them in a dark, warm place. They are ready to strip off their stems and put in jars or combine into blends when they are papery and rustly-dry to the touch. Make your own potpourri from dried flowers and herbs from your own garden.

And don't forget, this is a *hot* month. Remember to water your plants deeply in the morning.

SEPTEMBER:

The Seeking Moon

LETTUCE SOWN LATE,
TOMATOES GALORE,
CUT-AND-COME-AGAIN GIVES US MUCH MORE.

Lots of plants love to be cut and used, cut and used again. Plant a pot of lettuce. When the plants are 3 or 4 inches high, trim enough of the outer leaves to make a salad. In a couple of weeks the lettuce will have forgotten this assault and grown back. You'll be able to keep cutting it right up til the first frost.

When you harvest corn, leave some ears on the stalks for

autumn bouquets or door decorations. Harvest whole heads of sunflowers for the birds. Let them dry in a garage or shed, but better hang them high or the mice will get all the seeds.

You can make a simple sunflower wreath by cutting out the center of the seedhead before it gets hard and dry. The birds love these!

The Leaf-Falling Moon

IN THE DARK I AM SEEKING NEW GEMS FOR MY CROWN;
WE WILL DREAM OF GREEN LEAVES WHEN THE
WOODS TURN BROWN.

—LUCY LARCOM

If you live in an area that has cold winters, you need to put your rosemary and bay tree into pots and bring them indoors for the next few months.

Look for rose hips. String some on thread to make garlands.

Gourds should be ready for harvest. Knock on them; do they sound solid? Wipe them off, dry them in a warm, protected, airy place, turning them every few days. When they're completely dry, you can wax them.

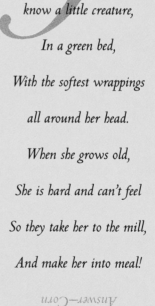

I know a little creature,

In a green bed,

With the softest wrappings

all around her head.

When she grows old,

She is hard and can't feel

So they take her to the mill,

And make her into meal!

Answer—Corn

HERE IS STRAWBERRY POPCORN

TIME TO USE THE BUNCHES OF HERBS YOU GATHERED AND DRIED LAST SUMMER.

YOU CAN MAKE SIMPLE GIFTS OF WREATHS AND PRESSED FLOWER PICTURES.

The Ice-Forming Moon

CLEAN AND ROUND,
HEAVY AND SOUND,
INSIDE EVERY BULB
A FLOWER IS FOUND!
—OLD POEM

On November 6, go outside and find a sleeping hawthorne, apple, or lilac. Cut a long branch, put it in a vase, and keep it warm. Watch for blooms. If it blooms by Christmas, you will have good luck in the new year.

Buy some narcissus bulbs. Spread pebbles on the bottom of a shallow dish. Put the bulbs in bottoms down. Add enough water to cover the pebbles and to just reach the bottoms of the bulbs. Put them in a dark spot and wait. Don't forget to add water from time to time.

If you live in a mild climate it is not too early to begin planning and planting for your summer tent of hollyhocks. Fill 5- or 6-inch pots with good, rich soil. Plant 4 or 5 hollyhock seeds in each pot and water daily. Once they are up and going, give them a handful of compost and an occasional feeding of fish emulsion.

The Long Night Moon

BIRDS AND CHILDREN
LIKE TO GO
WHERE THE BERRIED HOLLIES GROW.

Bring the narcissus bulbs out into the light, add more water, and give each a gentle tug to strengthen the roots. They will grow taller rapidly and soon be blooming, filling the room with their intense perfume.

Hyacinth bulbs that have been chilling in the refrigerator since mid-autumn can be potted in soil or set in hyacinth vases. Fill vases with water just to where the necks of the vases narrow, set a bulb pointed-end up in each, and place in the dark until lots of roots have formed and the bulbs have sent up short spears of green. Then move them to a sunny spot, where they will bloom after the first of the year.

After narcissi and hyacinths finish blooming, let them turn completely brown before you cut off the leaves. The leaves send nutrients back to the bulbs to store food for the next season. Plant them in pots of soil or set them out in the garden; they might bloom again next year.

If an onion wears

three coats of skin,

A long, hard winter

will soon set in.

Hollyhock Days

CHAPTER THREE

DEAR OLD GARDEN OF LONG AGO,

PART OF MY CHILDHOOD MEMORIES,

HOLLYHOCKS NOD IN YOUR FARTHEST ROW

UNDER THE LINDEN TREES.

— BESSIE SHERMAN

The Hollyhock Hermit

My Grandmother Lovejoy always told me that hollyhocks and humans love to "keep company" with each other. She said that hollyhocks never just naturalize along roadsides and meadows the ways fennel and chicory do. Hollyhocks crowd next to porches, peer into windows, line pathways and walls, and stay pretty close to home.

I was thinking of that years ago when my friend and I were walking deep into a canyon in the California hills. We were busy skipping flat stones across pooled areas of a creek, and we kept trying to scare each other with stories of mountain lions attacking. Then, I looked around and realized that the manzanita and toyon and ceanothus (these are a sort of wild lilac) were surrounded by towering 8- and 10-foot walls of hollyhocks. Hollyhocks lined the creek, hollyhocks flanked the trail. I couldn't figure it out. Hadn't Grandmother told me they wouldn't go out and live in the wild like other plants? She said they needed the companionship of humans. How could this be?

We kept walking along the trail and made a turn and the path widened into a steeply walled box canyon. We peered up at the brilliant, blue sky and saw hollyhocks of every imaginable color (one was so dark it looked black) hugging all of the narrow ledges to the very top of the canyon.

The rainbow of hollyhocks stood out against the pink sandstone and blue sky. I'll never forget the sound of buzzing from the bumblebees and the zipping and scolding of hummingbirds busily chasing each other. We laughed as a fat bumblebee chased a hummingbird away from a cupped, pink blossom, and the hummingbird turned and dive-bombed a huge hawk sitting on a toyon branch at the top of a cliff.

All of a sudden we froze and covered our mouths to muffle our laughter. Halfway up the stone face of the canyon on a wide, protected ledge, we saw an old man in tattered clothes. He was sitting in a broken-down chair in the middle of some sort of a shadow-striped room, hand feeding and talking to a Steller's jay and a squirrel.

"Look!" I whispered. "His tent is all hollyhocks. The same hollyhocks we followed up the trail. I told you that they only live around people." Each stripe in the tent was composed of groups of hollyhocks all of one color. First would be a stripe of about a dozen yellow hollyhocks, then a dozen pink, a dozen peach, and so on. About 8 feet up the stalks of the plants, he had pulled them together and tied them with thin rope. In a way it looked like an Indian encampment up on that ledge. Instead of smoke pouring from the top of a tepee, there were spills and spikes of toppling, bee-filled hollyhocks.

We must have made a noise because the Steller's jay cocked his head and screeched at us as he flew away. The old man jumped up and grabbed some sort of a cane or stick and started shaking it at us and yelling at us, "Go away! Get off my property!" He scram-

GIVE FOOLS THEIR GOLD,

AND KNAVES THEIR POWER;

LET FORTUNE'S BUBBLE

RISE AND FALL;

WHO SOWS A FIELD,

OR TRAINS A FLOWER,

OR PLANTS A TREE,

IS MORE THAN ALL.

—*John Greenleaf Whittier*

THE HOLLYHOCK FAIRY

*There's a sleepy little fairy that
lives in hollyhocks*

*She is waiting for the striking of
all the summer clocks.*

*Her little window-blinds are
drawn, of yellow, pink, and red,*

*And her little wings are folded
around her little head.*

*She is dreaming of the summer
and the coming of the bees,*

*Of the warmth within the garden
and the blossoms on the trees.*

—M. D. Cole, Saint Nicholas
Magazine, 1892

*Hollyhocks crowd
next to porches,
peer into windows,
line pathways
and walls . . .*

bled down from his room, and we took off running. We jumped rocks, leapt over the narrows of the creek, and slipped down rough, poison oak-covered animal trails.

By the time we reached home we were streaked with mud and leaves, the first evening star was out, and the poison oak blisters were already rising. Mother took one look at me and said, "Fels-Naptha soap, a cold shower, a cold dinner, and then to bed." I sure didn't mention the hollyhock hermit who talked to the animals and who chased us down from his wild gardens. A year later as Mother sat reading her morning paper she said, "Can you imagine that?! Some old hermit has been living up in the mountains for years on federal land. He was way up in a canyon and some rangers came upon him by accident. It says that he was a big-time rodeo star who was seriously injured. He was hospitalized, and when he was released he disappeared. I guess, according to the rangers, he didn't want to be around people anymore, just animals and flowers." Mother gulped down another sip of coffee and shook her head, "Do you see, dear, why I never want you traipsing around these wild mountains alone?

Hollyhock Tent

It is very easy to grow a hollyhock tent from seed. Trace a big circle in a flat, weed-free sunny spot. (Leave an opening for the door.) Step inside and sit down; make enough room in the circle for you and a few friends. With a trowel, a hoe, or your favorite kitchen spoon, follow your traced line and dig out a small trench a few inches deep. Make sure the soil in your trench is loose so that the small seeds of hollyhocks can easily sprout. Add some of the compost from your "possibilities" pile. (If you are transplanting hollyhock seedlings make sure the trench is deep enough for the long roots.)

Drop in a couple of hollyhock seeds ½-inch deep every 12 inches all the way around the circle. Don't forget to leave that door! If you started hollyhocks outside in pots in November or in peat pots in January you have a head start. Gently transplant them 12 inches apart all around your tent. Give them a good handful of your worm-rich compost and fertilize with fish emulsion. (You can thin or transplant extra hollyhocks later if they are too crowded.) If you want a striped tent like the one the Hollyhock Hermit lived in, you will have to separate the colors into groups of about ten of each hue.

Every day, (unless it rains) you must go out and make sure that your circle is moist. After a couple of months, when your hollyhocks are about 5 feet high, gather all of the tops together like a big bouquet. You can use a thin rope or thick twine and tie the stalks loosely together. Now you have a tent like the one the Hollyhock Hermit lived in. The hollyhocks will reappear and keep growing in your magical circle for years to come. If your hollyhock leaves have rusty orange spots on them, pick off the diseased leaves. The beautiful Painted Lady and the West Coast Lady butterflies adore this plant! Hummingbirds and bumblebees will be constant visitors, too.

HOLLYHOCKS NEVER FAIL to delight the eyes. But they delight the palate, too. The blooms can be stuffed with cream cheese, guacamole, or any number of sour cream dips. For a special birthday party, we fill each hollyhock bloom with scoops of sherbet or ice cream. Did you know you can eat the cheeses, which is an old-fashioned name for the seed pods? I eat green cheeses all the time. I cook them in a little bit of oil and add them to salads. Or I harvest the dried, brown cheeses full of seeds. I separate the colors and dry the seeds for the next year's planting. Sometimes I dry extra seeds for gifts or to trade. I have hollyhock seeds that have been sent to me from all over the world. Some seeds come from gardens more than 200 years old!

aurie Archer wrote me this letter about her childhood play with hollyhocks:

"I do have the most delightful memories of long and elaborate hollyhock doll weddings. The men always got short shrift here, for it is rather difficult to make a boy hollyhock doll, unless you know something I don't. We have a yard full of hollyhocks, and I seem to remember they were only the single variety, no show-off doubles or special hybrids or variegated ones. And I think, as an aside, that the term *alley-orchid* was applied to them.

"The setting for all this ritual and dreams was an old peach tree in Danville, Kentucky, in the late 1930s and early 1940s. My peach tree had conveniently let itself grow four low branches that of course made my job easier of dividing them up into rooms.

"I would pick the largest white hollyhock blossom for the bride, leaving a short stem for the neck. To make the head, I would

For a long lasting bouquet of hollyhocks, singe the bottoms of

punch a hole in the side of an unopened bud and stick it on the neck stem. One could tilt these heads in a number of ways to provide more haughty or slightly askew bridesmaids if one wished.

"Then, I would attach a large petal to the point of the head bud to provide a wimple-like drape. I think I had seen many books of the medieval period with that kind of costume. These would be fastened with little bits of twigs, or whatever else was handy to get the job done.

"The processions got out of hand with sometimes as many as twenty-five bridesmaids in gowns from pink to the darkest purple. A neighbor boy, little Dicky Parks, used to help and be very involved in this, too. I've always wondered if he turned out to be a dress designer.

the flower stalks with a candle; then put in a vase of fresh water.

"The groom was usually a string doll. Plain old wrapping twine, wound around a small hand to sufficient fatness, then tied, then cut until you had a semblance of a figure.

"The receptions were also elaborate. Still under the peach tree, we would find enough split-open peach pits so everyone could have a dish. We had a gooseberry bush that provided many a main course. Once in a while the family rooster would be in residence, so one or the other of us would have to stand guard armed with the broom to fend him off from our activities."

THE BRIDE WORE WHITE

Hideaways and Quiet Places

CHAPTER FOUR

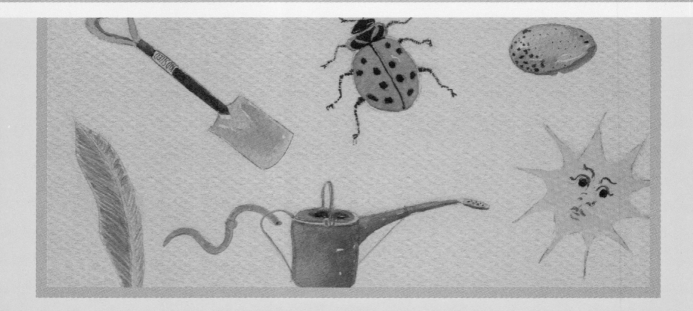

I'D LOVE TO FIND MY OWN QUIET NOOK,

WHERE I COULD CURL UP WITH A BOOK,

AND KNOW THAT THE

ONLY THINGS WATCHING ME

WERE THE BIRDS AND THE BUGS AND AN OCCASIONAL BEE.

MOST BUTTERFLIES LIVE VERY SHORT LIVES; BUT THE MONARCH BUTTERFLIES, HANGING LIKE SHINGLES FROM MY EUGENIA TREE, LIVE ALMOST NINE MONTHS. THE MONARCH IS THE LONGEST-LIVED BUTTERFLY.

&veryone needs time and a place alone. I think natural playhouses and hideouts are the best. A place to think or not to think, to read, to dream. A place to watch bees and butterflies, to listen to the wind (or the fairies) whisper in the trees and compliment the flowers, and to hear the songs of birds and insects. Children and adults alike need a special place, a hideaway, to spend time with the most important person in their lives—themselves.

Trees make some of the best hideaways where you can be alone but never lonely. The ancient Greeks believed that in every tree lives a dryad, a beautiful forest nymph. The dryad was born with the tree and died the moment the tree's life ended. The Greeks listened to the voices in the trees. They knew that the dryads played and sang in the rustling, leafy branches.

IN THE LANGUAGE OF FLOWERS, THE MULBERRY IS THE SYMBOL OF WISDOM.

In 1827 while visiting Old Salem, North Carolina, Julia Margaret Connor stumbled upon a unique and beautiful summer playhouse, unlike any she had seen before. Eight giant cedar trees were planted in a circle. When the trees were young they had been chained together at the center and the branches all trimmed neatly to form walls. A small area was cut through to form an entryway.

As the years passed the cedars were kept trimmed to a height of about 8 feet. The cedar bough walls became thicker and thicker as time passed. So thick, in fact, that wide window seats were cut into the walls—real window seats that you could actually sit on!

My friend Gerry Bullington Bauman, owner of the Farmhouse Herb shop in Grimes, Iowa, grew up in Saylorville, Iowa, just outside of Des Moines. The best playhouse she ever had was a 20-foot wide old lilac that grew in her grandparents' yard. She and her sister Janet played inside the big empty center of the huge, old bushes. She still remembers the wisteria and spirea that surrounded the lilacs.

Pliny the Elder, a naturalist who lived from A.D. 23 to 79, observed, "The mulberry tree was esteemed the wisest of all trees because it never expanded its buds until all fear of frost was past."

Lilactide is what children called spring a hundred years ago. It was believed that the perfume of the lilac was strong enough to guard homes from the Evil Eye. Have you ever noticed how many lilac bushes grow beside cottage doors?

THERE IS A SEMI-DWARF MULBERRY TREE AVAILABLE THAT GROWS TO ABOUT 15 FEET TALL AND 15 FEET WIDE. NICE SIZE FOR A HIDEOUT! THE GARDEN GUIDES TELL ME THAT THE MULBERRY CAN GROW IN A CLIMATE THAT GETS DOWN TO 7 DEGREES BELOW ZERO.

"Miss Lovejoy, could you take a few minutes to come and see my secret hideout?" a tall gentleman in work clothes asked quietly. He introduced himself to me as Houston Knight, one of the hard-working volunteers at the Fullerton Arboretum in Fullerton, California.

He led me to a huge black mulberry tree. The leafy branches of the mulberry tree formed a great mound that swept clear to the ground.

"Duck your head over here, and bend down; now scoot inside." I crouched and crawled through a break in the wall of leaves that was hardly noticeable. No wonder Houston's hideout was such a secret!

Once inside the canopy of huge leaves and branches both of us were able to stand up, and Houston must be well over six feet tall. Large, swooping boughs provided perfect seats and perches inside of the hideout. But that wasn't all. Houston said, "Now, close your eyes, and open your mouth, and don't be afraid to eat what I'm going to feed you." I guess I really trusted him because he could've dropped stink bugs down my throat if he had wanted!

I felt two warm, squashy objects on my tongue. Maybe he *was* feeding me stink bugs! I opened my eyes and chomped down. Houston said, "Aren't they great? They're mulberries." He was right, they were great—sort of like soft, mild blackberries. Houston was holding a couple more of the plump, maroon berries and popped them into his mouth. "Don't try to eat them when they're green," he said. "Only when they're this deep color."

For my birthday this year my mother bought me a beautiful Persian black mulberry. Already seven feet tall, it is in a huge pot and waiting to be planted. I have named my tree "Houston" and will think of him every time I hide away in my mulberry.

What's Wattle?

Long ago, before the invention of the chain link fence or barbed wire, farmers and gardeners had to figure out how to keep free-roaming animals from eating their gardens and orchards. They made their own fences with natural things available to them. They roamed along creeks and cut long branches of willow (and anything else they could use) to bring home.

They soaked the willow rods—called osiers—until they would bend easily, and then they wove them in and out of slender fence posts set close together. This kind of fence was called wattle. The wattle fences protected vegetable gardens, fruit trees, herb gardens, anything that might be damaged by wandering swine or clumsy cows.

It is easy to make your own wattle fence. You can even make tiny fences to surround doll houses or miniature flower gardens, but why just stop at a fence? Make a playhouse or a wigwam. Stick long, smooth stakes into the ground in a circle, then weave in and out, around and around, with long willow rods that you've soaked in water.

In the olden days a willow wand was hung over the door as protection from all evil influences and illness. Just think of the good luck you could have living in a willow wigwam!

THE STRANGE
MUSIC TREE

In Africa tiny insects are born in long thorns on branches white as chalk. When the insects chew their way out of the thorns, they leave little holes behind in the thorns. When the wind whistles through the leafless branches a musical noise comes from each of the hollow thorns, like thousands of flutes or piccolos being blown at once. The Africans call these "whistling trees".

My Friend

Kids climb, bees hive,

Bats roost, spiders spin,

Raccoons hide, swings dangle,

Rain drips, bugs chew,

Birds nest, squirrels jump.

Days dapple, nights unfold,

and spread a

star- flecked coverlet

over my friend,

My Tree.

Laughing Willows: Living Chairs

Michael Emmons is an artist who lives in a home precariously perched on a high mountain hugging the ocean in Big Sur, California.

Michael works with willow to make beautiful, unique furniture—not ordinary willow furniture, but furniture that is living and growing. His business is called Laughing Willows, and laugh is just what I did when I saw his living willow chair.

Michael cut and soaked willow rods, and bent and wove them together to make a grand high-backed chair. He put his chair into the bed of a truck and moved it several thousand feet up the mountain, setting it on a hill with a view that stretched forever.

A day or so after Michael put his chair on the mountaintop, it began to rain lightly. Then, more and more rain pounded down on the mountain and the lonely willow chair. A few weeks passed and if you looked closely you could see the tiniest green leaflets just beginning to appear along the four legs of the chair. In another month the chair had taken firm hold of the earth again, roots stretched down into the soil. Leaves and twigs totally covered the legs of the chair, and there were even some pussy willow buds!

Months later, on a visit to the top of Willow Chair Mountain, we discovered a beautiful male kestrel (a small falcon) perched on the top rung of the chair's back. He sat like a king on a throne, barely turning his head to look at us before he took flight and hovered, flapping his wings rapidly, and dove to grab a tiny mouse. The kestrel quickly returned to his chair and ate his catch.

The willow chair had become a part of the huge mountain and lupine-covered hill that looked over the sparkling ocean, and it was the personal lookout perch for a fiercely beautiful falcon.

You can make a living willow chair by taking four long cuttings (or buying them at a nursery) and planting them in a square like chair legs. As they grow, train them into the arms, seat and back of a chair.

Gardens help teach us patience, and you will need patience to do this living chair project. It may take many months or even years.

GIVE ME THE GREEN GLOOM OF A LOFTY TREE

LEAF AND BOUGH TO SHUTTER AND BAR

MY DREAM OF THE WORLD THAT OUGHT TO BE.

FROM THE DRIFTING GHOSTS OF THE THINGS THAT ARE.

—*From* FEAST OF LANTERNS: THE SECRET LAND

On a roasting hot day, I sat in the welcomed shade of an exuberant passion vine that had twined and wound around every bit of an old, broken-down gazebo. Throughout the day the vine was  constant host to dozens of visiting butterflies and inquisitive kids. "Is that a butterfly vine?" one boy asked after he had been watching all of the winged activity for a half an hour.

"I guess it is sort of a butterfly vine," I told the young boy.

"They sure seem to love it," he said, nodding his curl-capped head.

That day under the passion flower vine really started me thinking. What if I made a caterpillar cave and planted it with lots of the plants caterpillars love to eat?

First I built a cave frame from wooden lath. Then I planted passion flower to attract the brilliant Gulf Fritillary, common in southern states and the middle states in summer. Some passion flowers are native to the eastern United States. They can freeze to the ground but make a comeback when the ground warms. When I look at a passion flower I always feel as if I am journeying through the tropics! Next, in went aristolochia (called pipevine because of the shape of its flowers). Aristolochia attracts the beautiful Pipevine Swallowtail, which can be found throughout most of the United States. There are many

Parsley, Dutchmen's breeches, and dill will entice Black Swallowtails.

other vines you can grow on a caterpillar cave; red admirals and hairstreaks especially love hops and sweetpeas.

My favorite ground cover is chamomile, so we planted a chamomile floor in the caterpillar cave. At the back of the cave we planted two bronze fennel plants. We chose bronze fennel, with its deep mahogany foliage, because it will get very tall, but not spread horizontally as Florence fennel does. It will be a willing host to bees and butterflies galore.

All along the sides of the cave we planted masses of flowers in all of the colors a butterfly likes. Parsley, Dutchmen's breeches, and dill will entice Black Swallowtails. My sunflowers really attracted a variety of butterflies and hummingbirds. I love buckeye butterflies; they look as if they're looking at you. Plant paintbrush for the buckeyes.

The first butterfly that visited the caterpillar cave and stopped to lay a few eggs really got the royal treatment. She deposited her eggs on the underside of a leaf. After she left I touched the eggs and they were actually glued on. Only a few days passed and the eggs turned from a light color to a dark grey. Soon the eggs hatched and out came my first hungry guest, with many more to follow.

Through the magnifying glass I watched every bite that first caterpillar took! When I blew on him, a couple of bright orange knobs called o*smeteria* would pop out. He would rear his head and act quite fierce. I must say, looking at him through the magnifying glass, he looked fierce, too!

Caterpillars eat plants,

Butterflies sip nectar.

Caterpillars eat day and night,

Butterflies feed during the day.

Moths usually feed from fragrant

white plants at night.

Butterflies love purple, lavender,

red, pink, orange, and yellow.

THE BUTTERFLY DIPPED,

And circled to smell

His floriferous dinner,

Which suits him quite well.

BUT WHERE IS HIS SNIFFER?

You may ask when we meet.

His antennae,

Proboscis,

And even his feet!

BUT, WAIT JUST A MINUTE!

My story's not through.

His feet have more talents—

He tastes with them, too!

I also found out that what caterpillars do most and best is eat and poop, with four or five short time-outs for molting during their life as a hungry caterpillar. (The growing periods between molts are called *instars*.)

At the end of the caterpillars' last instar, they began a clumsy search for a safe and sheltered spot. Then, another miracle took place as I lay stretched out on chamomile, with paper and watercolors in hand.

They spun chrysalises, the silky cocoon cases they live in while they turn into adult insects. Cocoon comes from an old French word meaning shell. Chrysalis comes from the word *chrysos*, which means "golden sheath of a butterfly". Chrysalises are really vulnerable. I watched anxiously as the jays picked and pecked at my cave.

When the first chrysalis split, the butterfly—at least it was supposed to be a butterfly—emerged slowly. Gosh, it was a wreck! It looked worse than I do when I haven't slept for a day or two.

The butterfly struggled out onto a twig and slowly pumped fluid into its wrinkled wings. Finally, after what seemed like ages, my first butterfly took a leisurely cruise around the butterfly flowers.

Butterflies are most comfortable with flowers big enough to land on. They need a feeding platform, unlike hummingbirds or hawkmoths, which hover. Watch the butterflies feeding. Their proboscis is like a double straw.

Pull out your magnifying glass and look closely at the last plant a butterfly visited. Do you see little lines of patterns leading into the center of the flower? Those are called nectar guides, a sort of treasure map for the butterflies to follow straight into the center of the flower where the nectar is waiting.

Some nectar guides are invisible to us, but not to the butterflies. You can bet that if one of your flowers is frequented by butterflies it has nectar guides, invisible or not.

> Don't pull out nettles, but watch them closely.
>
> You will see lots of caterpillars
>
> chewing on them.

PLANTS FOR BUTTERFLIES AND CATERPILLARS

Asters

Borage

Carrots

Chicory

Cosmos

Hollyhocks (of course)

Knapweed

Milkweed

Mugwort

Parsley

Peppermint

Pearly Everlasting

Phlox

Sedum (these blooms are always alive with butterfly activity)

Snapdragons

Thistle

Verbena

Violets

Plant World Curiosities

CHAPTER FIVE

My grandma used to say to me

A garden was the place to be

When I was overcome by doubt

And showed a tendency to pout;

A place where any troubled child

Could find, in colors running wild

And fragrances to soothe the soul,

The balm to make his spirit whole.

— From "Snippets and Snails and Curious Tales"
ARTHUR FREDERIC OTIS

Gardens shouldn't be all serious and hard work. You need to relax and even have a good chuckle among your plants. Mother Nature has a sense of humor. If you do grow some of Her curiosity plants, people may ask how did you ever do *this*? You can answer knowingly that you had a little help from Mother.

The long walking stick cabbage is also the mythical stick that Irish fairies ride instead of horses. In Scotland, when a young girl pulls up a kale to cook, she strips off the leaves, one at a time, naming the names of three of her male friends. One is for John, two is for Joe, three is for Jack, four is for John, five is for Joe, six is for Jack, over and over until she reaches the last leaf. If the last leaf is the name of someone she doesn't want as a sweetheart, she has to forego eating the soup she prepares, or she will end up marrying him!

Great cow cabbage, long jacks, tree cabbage, coles, cole-wort, and long wortes. These are all names for the fascinating "walking stick" cabbage plant. The Latin names are *Brassica oleracea* (a wild variety) and *Brassica oleracea longata* (the one that's listed in seed catalogs.

Eugene Kociba, horticulturist at the Fernwood Botanic Garden in Niles, Michigan, brought the plant to my attention in a letter.

"We have a walking stick cabbage patch where cabbage plants grow up to 5 feet tall by the end of season, at which time the leaves are stripped off and the stalks left to dry. After drying they can be varnished and used for walking sticks," he wrote.

At the end of the letter he promised to send me a walking

Nature has a sense of humor

stick as soon as it was ready to be harvested. While I was waiting, I spent hours researching the old "long jack". Can you imagine a cabbage so tall that its gets to be the size of a small tree? When Darwin traveled to the Channel Islands of England, he recorded wild cabbages reaching heights up to 16 feet. It is not unusual to find them from 12 to 15 feet tall, but I think the record holder is 20 feet—as tall as a two-story building! This cabbage is so big that it has been used as rafters to support the roof of a house.

When I received a tall, narrow box from Fernwood, I dragged it to my tiny upstairs office and eagerly opened it. Phew!

MIRACLES

The office went from being sweetly fragrant to incredibly stinky. Eugene had sent me one of his walking stick cabbages, leaves, roots, and even a bit of soil.

Eugene says that the walking stick cabbage will grow and thrive in most soils. Cabbages do love moisture and cool weather, so you can plant it in early spring or fall. Allow a couple of feet of growing space for each plant.

To get straight stalks you have to stake the plants as they grow, but Eugene likes to let them twist and turn and hunch. He thinks that they have much more personality that way. When the stalk starts to get a couple of inches thick, start stripping off the lower leaves. When the plant reaches the height you want, pull it out of the ground, roots, head and all, and hang it in a barn, garage, or potting shed, somewhere dry and airy. (Remember, it smells like brussels sprouts cooking.) Let it dry for a couple of months. By the time it is thoroughly dry, it will be very lightweight.

Poke a hole through the very top and thread it with a piece of rawhide for a handle. Or just leave it as is and give the stick a coating of varnish. Let it dry thoroughly. And if your roof rafters need repair, there is always that huge cabbage that just keeps growing and growing and growing.

Everyone has heard all the rules about growing good carrots. You must have sandy soil. You must space the seeds just so. You can't have any lumps and pebbles in the ground. And so on. I have some different ideas about that. Growing carrots my way is one of the easiest garden projects I know, and and especially fun for children.

First, of course, you'll need seeds. If you think a carrot is just a carrot, you will be in for a surprise when you start looking at how many kinds of seed are available from garden centers and catalogs—'Nantes', 'Caramba', 'King Midas', 'Little Finger', 'Thumbelina', 'Baby Long', 'Belgian White'—and lots more. Some of these are long and skinny, some short and chubby, and some are almost as round as radishes. They come in all the colors of the sunset, from pale creamy gold to deep red-orange. Some even revert back to their original purple. Children will have a lot of fun deciding which ones to get, but no matter which ones they choose for their carrot caper, they'll taste better than the ones from the store, which are so often bitter or woody.

When children open a packet of seeds, they're often surprised to see how tiny they are. It's hard to imagine those wee specks growing into long, fat, orange snacks!

"Two Carrots in Love" is drawn from a photograph by Betty Cerar of Palgrave, Ontario, Canada. Betty sent the photo to Organic Gardening Magazine *and lots of people got a chuckle out of it.*

CARROTS COME IN

For your carrot farm, use a big pot, a half-barrel, or a little plot in the garden. Add plenty of compost, plus pebbles and rocks. That's right, pebbles and rocks . . . and clods and gravel, too. Not just on top of the soil, but mixed all through it.

At this point, veteran vegetable gardeners are probably muttering to themselves, "She sure doesn't know how to plant carrots. Anyone knows that you have to get rid of rocks and pebbles and clods or the carrots won't grow straight." But wait a minute—who's to say what's proper for a carrot?

Sprinkle the carrot seeds all over this rich, rocky soil, and just barely cover them with it. Then water the soil gently but thoroughly. Someone will have to make sure the soil doesn't dry out during the time that the first roots and shoots are forming.

In a few weeks, there will be a small forest of two-inch carrot tops all over the pot or plot. They're sure to be too crowded, so next comes the hard part—thinning them out. These "victims", tiny as a snip of thread, are already great tasting, or they can be put to good use in the compost pile.

A L L   S H A P E S   &   S I Z E S

To help the remaining carrots along, this is a good time to apply fish emulsion fertilizer. This smelly concoction, available from most garden centers, is mixed with water and poured around the edges of the pot, if that's how you're growing your carrots, or around their roots. Remind children that even a "natural" fertilizer shouldn't be poured on the plants' leaves!

After a few more weeks, the plants will begin to look big and feathery on top. Children—and maybe their adult helpers as well—may become curious about what's going on underground. There's no rule that says they can't peek. Have them grab one of the carrot tops close to the ground and tug gently. With luck, they'll find that carrot capers are underway.

Because of those rocks and pebbles and clods that you mixed with the soil, you won't find the kind of neat, straight, boring carrots that come from the store. Instead, you'll find dancing, bending, twisting carrots, no two alike. You might find a carrot with two "legs", or even three, or a carrot sitting down, or two carrots in love and dancing cheek to cheek.

The only problem with growing carrots this way is that they have so much personality, you might not want to eat them.

NANTES

•

NANTES HALF-LONG

•

NANTES TIP TOP

•

NAPOLI

•

PLANET

•

RED-CORED CHANTENAY

•

SUCRAM

•

SWEETNESS

•

THUMBELINA

•

TOKITA'S SCARLET

•

TOUCHON

Before we had neighborhood supermarkets,

efore we had neighborhood supermarkets, hardware stores, and lumber yards, brooms grew in gardens. Take a look at that broom you have in your closet. If it isn't made of plastic, just what is that stuff you see at the end? Chances are you are looking at the tops of broom corn. Long ago, the broom plant was grown and harvested still on its long stalk. Several stalks were bound together with twine to form a handle. The broom bristles looked like a big bouquet. Years passed and someone thought of cutting the bristles off and attaching them to a wooden handle. The brooms were attached with wire, leather, or twine, but they were still very crude, round, hard-to-use bundles.

The Shakers of Watervliet, New York, are credited with inventing the first flat broom as we know it today. The Shakers invented furniture and tools that were not only beautiful but functional. A flat broom is indeed functional.

Records from an 1836 journal in New Lebanon, New York, mention that Brother Orren Haskins turned out 1,000 brooms in one day. That's either a lot of brooms or an extremely long day! Some of the catalogs that I have listed in the back of the book carry broomcorn seeds. Plant seeds when your soil is warm, about the same time you'd plant sweet corn or field corn. After your first sprouts are up, lay mulch around them. I planted a patch of Hungarian broom corn one year, and it produced beautiful sprays of red tops.

Your broom will take about 100 to 110 days before it is ready to harvest. On a clear, dry day, when the broom tops are ready—right after the bloom fades but before the seeds ripen and become brittle—make a cut partway through each stalk about 3 feet down from the head (or however long you want the handle to be). Bend the tops over at the cut so that they rest on each other, making sure they don't touch the ground. This is the ancient practice in harvesting called *tabling*. Step back; it will look like a table once all of your broom tops are bent. If you want a whisk broom, just cut the stalks shorter!

I have seen broom corn grown in old produce boxes, barrels, and pots. I've seen them grown as a tall privacy fence between homes and as a simple maze—no pun intended—in a back yard.

. . . BROOMS GREW IN GARDENS

Pot o' Broom

FIRST YOUR LUFFA'S JUST A SPROUT,

THEN IT'S UP,

AND CLIMBING ALL ABOUT.

NOW YOUR LUFFA HAS A FLOWER,

FEED IT SOME FISH,

IT WILL MAKE YOU A BOWER.

NOW YOUR LUFFA'S

TURNING YELLOW,

TIME TO HARVEST

THIS CAPRICIOUS FELLOW.

SPROUTING, CLIMBING,

FLOWERING YELLOW,

NOW IT'S A SPONGE.

UNPREDICTABLE FELLOW.

In some countries, luffa is called the rag gourd; in others, it is the vegetable sponge; still others call it the dishcloth squash or California okra. Whatever you want to call it, a luffa by any other name is still a luffa. (Or maybe a loofah.)

If you have a fairly long growing season, you can grow this member of the squash family in your garden. You can eat the ripened fruits or you can make wash cloths out of them. Either way, you will need a sturdy trellis or fence and lots of sunshine. Luffas are hungry vines and will grow in a well-prepared, warm bed.

At the foot of a trellis or fence—something for your vines to grow on—make a small hill for your seeds. Soak the luffa seeds for 48 hours before you plant them. To get an early start, plant each seed in a peat or plastic pot four or more weeks before the last frost date.

When the ground is warm, plant either three seeds or three plant sets in each hill. Cover the seeds with a half-inch of soil and keep them moist until they've germinated. Space your sponge hills at least 4 feet apart; the vines need plenty of space to roam!

Once your luffa is up and starts clambering over its fence or trellis, you must water it deeply and slowly early in the morning. Make sure that the soil is moist deep down into the hill. Give it a feeding of tomato fertilizer. You'll be rewarded with extra big and healthy sponges.

Now your vine is up and growing, covered with beautiful yellow flowers that will produce long, cucumber-like fruits. If you don't have a trellis or fence available, make a bed of mulch or of plastic for the fruits to rest on. You don't want them to rot on the wet soil.

As the fruits turn a light yellow, they are ripening right on the vine. If you look closely, you may see them breaking open, sort of unzipping their skins to reveal a spongy network of fibers inside.

When your luffas are fully ripe, pick them and put them in a big bucket or tub. Cover with water. (Add some Clorox to the water to kill any bacteria.) Leave them soaking for a few days. Check on them. Pretty soon the outer skin will start coming off in pieces. Peel off all of the skin; remove the pulpy, squashy part and any remaining black seeds. Anything gucky still sticking to the sponge can be removed under a stream of running water. Spread your sponges out on a bench or screen in the sunshine to dry out. When they're ready to use, they will have turned a lighter color.

Luffas are great. Take one in to the bath or shower and scrub your rough elbows and heels. Give them as gifts with floral soaps or herbs for hot baths.

Rag gourd
vegetable sponge
dishcloth squash
l u f f a

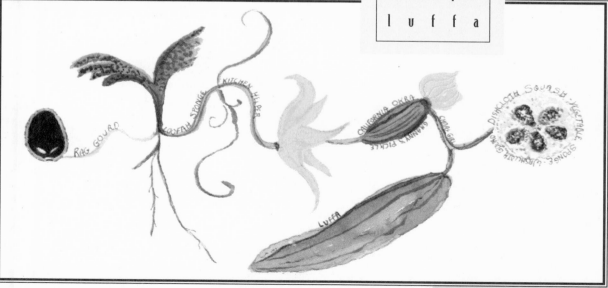

BUTTERFLY
Butterfly orchid
(*Oncidium papilio*)

CATERPILLARS
Scorpiurus vermiculatus

CENTIPEDES
Nardus stricta

DOVE
Dove orchid (*Peristeria elata*)

GRASSHOPPERS
Sterile oats (*Avena sterilis*)
Also referred to as animated oats
because of the odd behavior of the
seed that will twist about when
exposed to moisture or dryness

SNAILS
Medicago scutellata

SPIDERS
Spider orchid (*Phragmipedium* sp.)

SWANS
Swan orchid (*Cycnoches* sp.)

WORMS
Astragalus hamosus.

Snails in Your Soup, Worms in Your Salad

The straight-laced Victorians were wonderful gardeners and great pranksters. They devoted a lot of time to growing plants, both indoors and out. Many of the plants they loved were strange giants or carnivores like the meat-eating Venus flytrap. They enjoyed plants that looked like animals, birds, butterflies, or any number of insects.

I found a wonderful old picture of a bouquet made up of all plants that look like critters in an 1875 issue of *St. Nicholas Magazine.* Dr. Arthur O. Tucker, Delaware State College, acted as an informed detective and identified many of the plants pictured for me.

He also sent an article he had written on just this very subject, which describes plants that were grown, according to one eighteenth-century author, "for their oddness rather than any great beauty". They included:

CATERPILLARS——*Scorpiurus vermiculatus* and *S. muricatus*

SNAILS——*Medicago scutellata*

HORNS——*Cornucopiae cucullatum*

HEDGEHOGS——*Medicago intertestz*

HALF-MOONS——*Medicago arborea*

HORSESHOES——*Hippocrepis comosa*

Dr. Tucker says that plant "worms" were first mentioned in the 1849 seed catalog of Robert Cooper of Sion Nursery in England. Cooper listed "caterpillars, hedgehogs, snails, and worms for 3d per packet" under the heading of "hardy annuals". In 1943, another catalog mentioned that these horticultural worms, snails, and caterpillars were put into soups as "practical jokes".

"Doc's" Soup

FINGER PLAY

As an energetic child of five, the only way my Grandmother Lovejoy could still me was by playing familiar finger games. Don't you remember sitting with someone and playing *The Eensy Weensy Spider?* Or, how about, Here is the church, here is the steeple, open the door and see all the people? I remember that and often, when I am entertaining younger friends, I find that I am carrying on the storytelling tradition of finger-play taught me by my Grandmother.

Here is one for you to learn and play and pass on and on. . . .

The Little Plant

In my little garden bed *(make bed with hands)*
Raked so nicely over, *(indicate raking with fingers)*
First the tiny seeds I sow, *(sowing motions)*
Then with soft earth cover. *(covering motions)*
Shining down, the great round sun *(indicate sun with hands)*
Smiles upon it often;
Little raindrops, pattering down, *(patter with fingertips)*
Help the seeds to soften.
Then the little plant awakes!
Down the roots go creeping. *(point finger down and wiggle)*
Up it lifts its little head *(make fist and stick up thumb)*
Through the brown mould peeping.
Higher and higher still it grows
(keep thumb raised and lift arm higher and higher)
through the summer hours,
'Til some happy day the buds
Open into flowers.
(With hand raised open wide palm and fingers like an opening flower)

Wild Things

CHAPTER SIX

THE PINE TREE HAS ITS NEEDLES,

THE MAPLE HAS ITS KEYS,

THE ASH TREE'S SEEDS ARE PADDLES;

BUT TELL ME, WHAT ARE THESE?

NASTURTIUMS WITH UMBRELLAS

TO SHIELD THEM FROM THE LIGHT,

AND PITCHER PLANTS WITH PITCHERS

TO CATCH THE RAINDROPS BRIGHT.

THE ALDER WITH ITS TASSELS

WHICH GLEAM LIKE GOLDEN CURLS,

AND SASSAFRAS WITH MITTENS

FOR LITTLE BOYS AND GIRLS.

— "SASSAFRAS MITTENS"

You can make a cave for a

toad by turning a terra cotta

pot onto its side. Protect

toads from lawn mowers by

building hide-outs for them

(i.e., brush, rocks, wooden

boxes, etc.).

reatures both familiar and unfamiliar inhabit these pages. They bring enchantment to and create a healthy environment in the gardens, trees, ponds, and fields they call home.

In Defense of Toads

For two years I lived on the rim of a deep and winding canyon named Tecolote, after the owls that scoured it nightly with shrieks and screams and hungry eyes. Tecolote Canyon was a window to the wild world beyond our citified back yard. Foxes, coyotes, skunks, possums, raccoons, and bobcats would slink up to my tiny pond to drink. Birds of every size and color visited that life-giving pond, too. Once a pair of fiery-red cardinals (usually found in eastern gardens but not in ours out west) stopped by for a short stay.

Every evening in the spring, it became a tradition for our family to sit quietly by the side of a path leading to the pond. Crouching silently, not moving an eyelash, we peered down the busy sidewalk and watched our favorite evening procession under the newly lit street light.

Slowly, single file, a pair of handsome (in the toad world) western toads would walk awkwardly but resolutely to our driveway gate. Following the rut in the unpaved driveway, they would slip under the gate and amble down the hill to the pond.

The nighttime medley of cricket and frog calls would still suddenly, then begin again in chorus with the nasal song of the

The toad is never vicious,

Nor silly, nor stupid, nor slow.

Stupid? Perhaps you never

Noticed his jewel eyes?

Slow? Or his tongue's red lightning

Striking the darting flies?

No matter how stern and solemn

The markings about his eyes,

the width of his mouth preserves him

From wearing too grave a guise.

A hole in the ground contents him,

So little he asks of fate;

Philosopher under a dock-leaf,

He sits like a king in state.

FROM "A TOAD",
ELIZABETH AKERS ALLEN

toads. The lettuce and sweet peas were now safe at Seekhaven. Our toad friends would work diligently through the night, feasting on the slugs who had somehow escaped our twice daily garden patrol.

Early one morning, when I was checking on the welfare of the sweet peas, I glanced toward the pond and found long, clear ribbons of jelly, peppered with black-spotted eggs, floating on the water's surface. The toads had been busily laying eggs, and I was glad. Toads are like good books; you can't have too many.

In a few days hundreds of tadpoles hatched. During the following weeks the tadpoles went through their metamorphosis and gradually developed all of the characteristics of their handsome parents. I was ecstatic thinking of all of the good work the new platoon of toads would accomplish in my garden.

One rainy morning I walked down to the little pond. It was curiously still. Not a single tadpole remained. No matter where I looked—under chairs, between rocks, below raised planters—nowhere were there any new toads to be found, either.

That evening, as the sun finally slipped into the Pacific Ocean, we watched silently as a pair of handsome toads, and then another, and another, and another, walked solemnly down the sidewalk and headed toward the gardens. The frogs fell silent; the crickets stopped chirping. Some of the toads had come back to patrol our gardens. The rest of my toad children were out somewhere in our neighborhood, doing their garden guarding and slurping up succulent slugs. Do you think that any of my neighbors knew how lucky they were?

**Y**ou might just want to scream as a giant brown spider walks across the floor in front of you. But wait. Don't hurt that spider; look how small it is compared to you.

My cousin Margaret Macdonald taught me, "A good Scot never wastes anything, including a spider's life." So I learned from Cousin Margaret that a spider has a place in a home and a garden, just as we do.

Scientists have discovered that gardens are much healthier when they have a population of insect-eating spiders around. Those spiders you are shying away from are the very things keeping your garden plants happy and thriving. An ounce of spiders is worth a pound of pesticide!

The mulch we've created for our gardens is just the kind of home many of my favorite spiders are looking for. Your mulch of

grass clippings and composted leaves will make a nice, loose blanket over all of your beds. And your mulched beds are just what the spider needs. The mulch covering will provide a hideout with warmth, humidity, and lots of little critters for the spiders to eat.

Some of your spider guests may literally drop in for din-

SPIDERS SHOULD NEVER BE TAUNTED,
MALIGNED, ABUSED OR SCORNED—

THEY'RE HARD AT WORK IN OUR GARDENS—
JUST LOOK HOW THAT WEB IS ADORNED—

THE FILIGREED TATTING AND DEWDROPS
TELL TALES OF A HARDWORKING SPRITE—

AN ASSORTMENT OF BUGS,
SOME MOSQUITOES, A GRUB,
DON'T SPIDERS GET TIME OFF AT NIGHT?

ner—on silken balloons. Others may move from your neighbor's garden to yours because you have provided a safe and healthy habitat for them.

Spiders have lots of ways to trap their prey. Some spiders build complex webs that simply act as snares. Other spiders actually stalk their prey the same way a lion hunts.

Early in the morning or late at night go outside with a flashlight and look for all of the different webs the spiders have woven in your garden. Some will be shaped like huge, circular pieces of lace. (Touch one of the threads lightly, and you will alert the spider—who will zip out to investigate.) Other webs will be funnel shaped or a seemingly haphazard maze of threads running every which way. You may pass under a huge sheet web spread between the limbs of a tree. (I once found a hummingbird trapped in one of these.)

My favorite spider-built snare is the home of the trapdoor spider. Her home is a silk-lined tunnel with a hinged trap door. Open it and she'll rush up to the door and close it tightly. The trapdoor spider is a lazy hunter who simply waits for her victim to pass by; then, she grabs him and pulls him down into her tunnel.

R I D D L E

My first contains corn,
Or draws you and me;
You may call it a coin,
Or fowl of the sea,

My last may be coarse,
Or fine as a hair;
A membrane it is,
Or cloth that you wear.

My whole is a snare
Little insect, beware!

Answer: cobweb

Lady Bugs

A hundred years ago (maybe even today) it was believed that you would have nothing but good luck all day when a ladybird landed on you.

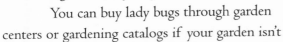

Those teeny, tiny critters called lady bugs have dozens of names. Cush-cow lady or Our Lady's ear, lady bird, lady beetle, barnaby bug, red turtle beetle, little spotted elfin cow, lady cow, and spotted tortoise-of-the-dell. Even the hungry larvae have the special name *aphid-wolf.* That is indeed what they are, feeding constantly on the aphids that can suck the life out of our plants. When I was young, I would pick up the little black and orange wolves and move them to any plant in the garden troubled by aphids. It is amazing how many they can eat.

You can buy lady bugs through garden centers or gardening catalogs if your garden isn't blessed by their presence. They'll come in a box, thousands upon thousands of orange-red lady bugs, and what a wonderful present they make! Most people make a big mistake when they get them. They open the boxes in the middle of the day and just let the lady bugs fly away. And fly away they do—right into the wind or their neighbors garden.

The lady bugs are looking for moisture. Wait until evening to release them. First, water the garden, and then let them out. Now they will have the moisture they need to settle down for the night.

Lady bird! Lady bird!
fly away home
Night is approaching,
and sunset is come;

The herons are flown
to their trees by the Hall;
Felt, but unseen,
the damp dewdrops fall;

This is the close
of a still summer day;
Lady bird! lady bird!
Haste! Flyaway!

OLD SONG

HUMMINGBIRD FACTS:

The bee hummingbird, which lives in Cuba, is the smallest bird in the world (2 and 1/4 inches)

■

Native Americans often refer to the hummer as the "rainbird". Desert plants flower soon after a rain storm, when the flowers bloom the hummers come, so the Native believed that the hummers brought the rain.

■

The rufous hummer should be called "the traveler". A rufous travels over 2,000 miles from its summer to winter home.

■

Hummers can fly upside down, yep, they can (for only short somersault and twist).

■

Hummingbirds have been clocked at 56 miles per hour!

■

Hummingbirds eat tiny insects.

■

On cold nights a hummer may lower his body temperature and enter a state of torpor almost like a hibernating animal. A female doesn't go into a torpor when she is incubating eggs; she stays warm, as do the eggs.

A Haven for the Hummers

The names of plants and birds and animals are usually easy to understand. As hummingbirds fly and hover, their wings hum. North American hummingbirds have names such as Black-chinned and Ruby-throated, which describe their colors and markings. The Berylline hummer is named after beryl, an emerald-green mineral or gem, the color of the hummer's brilliant feathers. But why in the world is a hummingbird named Lucifer? That name stems from the words *light-bringer* or *torch-bearer*. If you watch this rare, tiny traveler, you will see him brilliantly reflecting all the light of summer sunshine.

Hummingbirds have always been a part of my life. My earliest memories are of dueling, aggressive hummingbirds arguing loudly in the hollyhock patch of our garden. They spent their days divided between defending their hollyhock food source and dipping into the deep cups of bloom.

Hummingbirds are fearless, unless they get into an argument with a bumblebee. That is the only time I have ever seen them retreat! Hummers will dip down and visit you as you are watering your plants; they will investigate your shirt or shoelace if it is a bright color (they think it is food). They may perch on a feeder just as you are hanging it on a branch. The more time you spend out in your garden, the better your chances of sharing a moment with a hummer.

Last summer I spent hours under an Anna's hummingbird nest, and I got to know it quite well. One day, as I shook out an old red and white quilt and spread in on the ground, the Anna's zipped down to investigate what must have looked to her like a big flower bed. My quilt fascinated her. She totally ignored me and flew just inches above the edge of the quilt, until she reached a frayed corner with a fluff of filling sticking out. She stopped, dipped, grabbed the light filling in her long bill, tugged persistently, and flew off with a long streamer of fluff behind her. Deftly, she tucked the gauzy filling into her tiny nest. Then, she was back for more, pulling and tugging and teasing out bits and pieces. She spent the whole afternoon snitching lining for her nest—nineteen trips in all!

Hummers love to bathe. Often I see one of our hummers holding onto the very tip top of our fountain with his tiny feet. Wobbly, he dips in to the slight spray the fountain throws, wets his body, flutters tiny wings, dips again, and then flies swiftly away to dry in the sun. Early one morning a hummer flew to a large, pink hibiscus flower filled with rainwater and took a wild, splashing bath!

The day will come when they will recognize you when you fill their feeder!

-A hummer's tongue starts out as a tube, then splits into two tubes, like two thin straws.

-Hummers prefer tubular flowers. They are attracted to red, but sip from many colors.

-Hummers pollinate flowers.

-You may see hummers sticking their tongues into the holes made by sapsuckers and woodpeckers . . . they are probing for insects and taking advantage of the sap!

-Just at dusk, when other birds have retired, the hummer will be tanking up on food to sustain him through the night.

-Hummers use lots of cobwebs to build and line their nests and to fasten the nest to a branch.

-Hummers usually lay two long, narrow eggs, which the mother incubates.

THEY DRINK,

AND TAKE DIPS,

AND MAKE

ARDUOUS TRIPS.

THEY CAN HUM,

THEY CAN SIP,

YET THEY'RE MISSING

THEIR LIPS!

WHAT ARE THEY?

ANSWER: HUMMERS

You don't need lots of space or sunshine to have a hummingbird garden. It can be as small as a hanging pot of red and purple fuchsias or as large as a hillside planted with all of the flowers hummers love. Hummers love sugar water from feeders, too. They need to consume one-half of their daily body weight to survive. Remember to clean your feeder daily. Only use sugar and water; *no color, no honey.* Directions for sugar and water measurements will accompany your feeder. Follow feeder suggestions exactly!

Enjoy your little sky spirits. The day will come when they will recognize you when you fill their feeder!

HUMMERS CAN FLY UPSIDE DOWN

Other names for the hummer are PICAFLOR *(flower pecker),*
CHUPAFLOR *(flower sucker),*
BEIJA-FLOR *(Brazilian for flower kisser),*
AVES VARIAS *(many colored birds),* PAJARO MOSCA *(fly bird),*
TOMINEO *(little bit),* CHUPAROSA *(rose sucker),*
COLIBRI *(sky spirit),* CHUPAMEL *(honey sipper).*
The Aztecs called the hummingbird HUITZIL OR HUITZITZIL
(shining one with a weapon like a cactus-thorn).

Night's Nice

Every single evening, as I tucked my son Noah into bed, I would sing a song telling of the beauty and wonder of the night. I started the song with the words, "Night's nice." You see, Noah was afraid of the dark, and I wanted to reassure him, to let him know about all of the friendly creatures flying and chirping and hopping past his room as he slept peacefully and safely.

If you are lucky enough to live where you can see the stars, spread out a blanket and lie down and watch. Can you believe all of the shooting stars? On an ordinary night, if the sky is clear, you'll see several each hour. Look closely; sometimes you can see a rainbow completely circling the moon. I guess you would call it a moonbow!

Go on a nighttime exploration. Carry a flashlight and shine it into grass, bushes, and trees. Can you see eyes of all sizes shining back at you? Some may be the eyes of crickets, others of an owl. You can even see the tiny pinpoints of spider eyes. Look and listen. Can you hear the screech of a barn owl, the song of the whippoorwill, or a chorus of frogs? Are the larvae of the fireflies crawling hungrily, glowingly, along the ground?

Look for white flowers. They give up their fragrance to the night. Perhaps the white petunias are being visited by a huge, hovering moth. You can see why white flowers are so popular with the night flyers; they glow and shine, almost reflecting the moon. The fragrant, brilliant, red roses of the day are not even noticeable now. White claims the night!

Oh, Lady Moon, Your horns point toward the East Shine - be increased.

Oh, Lady Moon, Your horns point toward the West Wane - be at rest.

Christina G. Rossetti

Always Room for Bats

Although I love the dark, star-sugared night sky, I do enjoy turning on a bright light to attract moths. And moths attract bats. Find a street lamp or turn on the porch light. Stand back and watch the fluttering dance of the moths and the darting, dipping flight of the gentle bats, the sky weavers of night.

Bats have gotten a bad reputation when in reality they are helpers. Not only do they keep pesky insect populations down (they may each eat 3,000 insects a night), they help to pollinate many plants and disperse seeds. They are an important strand in the delicate web of life, helping to keep our gardens, forests, and deserts blooming. Here are a few facts to dispel the myths:

Bats are not blind, they have good vision. They won't get into your hair. They use their echolocation (bat sonar) to prevent things like that from happening. Bats aren't rodents; they're mammals, like us.

Save a spot in your hearts for the bats, and if you're lucky, they'll visit your garden and patrol your sky for insects. Bats are just another reason why night is nice.

My Friend Bombus

The Latin names of plants and animals are very descriptive. For instance, the Latin name for the bumblebee, *Bombus,* means "booming". If you lie down in the middle of a flower bed on a sunny afternoon when bumblebees are about and close your eyes, you will hear a sound almost as loud as a hummingbird's wings. It is a deep buzzing, almost booming.

Early morning, when the butterflies and bees are resting and waiting for the air to warm up, fuzzy bumblebees, clad in their own fur coats, get a head start on feeding. They shiver just like a person in the early morning waiting for someone to stoke up the fire. Bumblebees shiver to generate heat.

If you follow your bombus, you may find her visiting red clover. The bumblebee's long tongue is the only one that can reach deep into a clover bloom to sip nectar. Bumblebees love hollyhocks and snapdragons, too. Watch a bumble land on a snapdragon, a perfect host. If you have a patch of columbine that the bumblebees regularly visit, take some time to spy on the sipping bees. Sometimes a bumble will nestle deep into an older columbine bloom and one of the tubes will stick on the bee's head. The bumble will fly away wearing a colorful dunce's cap. She may not notice until she arrives home in a warm nest underground in some hole or burrow.

Your garden is a livelier, more interesting place when you make room for the wild things. Life is more meaningful when you share.

BUZZZ,

BUZZZ,

BUZZZ,

IS ALL YOU HEAR FROM

THE BUMBLING GOLD-BELTED

BUCCANEER.

Epilogue

It is winter now. The hollyhock days of summer seem so long ago. The only flowers blooming in my life are the narcissus and hyacinth filling my work room with fragrance.

It's time for me to finish this book, to say good-bye to you for awhile. I'll be piling mounds of garden catalogs up by my old red wing chair, and using my dogs as foot-warmers. I'll bundle up and plow through pages, circling that certain carrot or sunflower I can't live without.

I'll be building gardens in my mind and in my heart. When spring and my seed orders arrive, I'll be ready to start my seedlings, planning who will receive walking-sticks for gifts, how to furnish my hollyhock tent, and which wall will be best for my washing squashes.

Somewhere outside under a rock or planter, my favorite toad is resting. The gopher snake and king snake haven't shown their snouts for weeks. The bulbs are just breaking through their thick mulch coverlets, and the wild milk maids (the first wildflower of our new year) are starring the hillsides.

I'm anxious for spring and summer. Anxious to hear the laughter of children and the gentle clucking of the quail. But mostly, I am anxious for you to go outside and experience your garden. Remember to spend time listening, feeling, smelling, watching. Get to know a seed—they look so simple, and they are such amazing miracles. Watch which way plant tendrils twist; follow the bumblebee back to her nest; watch the caterpillars chewing through your caterpillar cave; squish good, dark mud through your toes. Hold these simple pleasures and mysteries close, and you will always have the secret recipe for childhood. When you are 85 years young, you will still be a child at heart—planting gardens and searching the night sky for a moonbow.

I wish for you every joy a garden can share.

Sharon

HOLD THESE

SIMPLE

PLEASURES AND

MYSTERIES

CLOSE

CATALOG SEED COMPANIES

Burpee Gardens, 300 Park Ave., Warminster, PA 18991-0001. (800) 888-1447, Fax (215) 674-4170.

Carroll Gardens, 444 East Main St., PO Box 310, Westminster, MD 21157. (800) 638-6334.

Cook's Garden, Box 65, Londonderry, VT 05148. (802) 824-3400.

Forestfarm, 990 Tetherow Rd., Williams, OR 97544-9599. (503) 846-6963.

Gardens Alive!, 5100 Schenley Place, Lawrenceburg, IN 47025. (812) 537-8650.

Gardener's Supply Co., 128 Intervale Rd., Burlington, VT 05401. (802) 863-1700.

Gurney's Seed & Nursery Co., 110 Capital St., Yankton, SD 57079. (605) 665-1930.

Hastings, 1036 White St. SW, PO Box 115535, Atlanta, GA 30310-8535. (800) 285-6580, Fax (404) 755-6059.

Heirloom Old Garden Roses, 24062 NE Riverside Dr., St. Paul, OR 97137. (503) 538-1576.

Henry Fields Seed & Nursery, 415 North Burnett, Shenandoah, IA 51602. (605) 665-9391.

Johnny's Selected Seeds, Foss Hill Rd., Abion, ME 04910. (207) 437-4301.

K. Van Bourgondien & Sons, 245 Farmingdale Rd., Route 109, PO Box A, Babylon, NY 11702-0598. (800) 552-9996, Fax (516) 669-1228.

Klehm Nursery, 4210 North Dunccan Rd., Champaign, IL 618210. (800) 553-3715.

Liberty Seed Co., PO Box 806, New Philadelphia, OH 44663. (216) 364-1611, Fax (216) 364-6415.

Lilypons Water Gardens, 6800 Lilypons Rd., PO Box 10, Buckeystown, MD 21717-0010. (800) 365-5459, Fax (800) 283-5459.

Logee's Greenhouses, 141 North St., Danielson, CT 06239. (203) 774-8038.

McClure & Zimmerman, 108 West Winnebago, PO Box 368, Friesland, WI 53935-0368. (414) 326-4220, Fax (414) 326-5769

Mellinger's, 2310 West South Range Rd., North Lima, OH 44452-9731. (216) 549-9861, Fax (216) 549-3716.

Milaeger's Gardens, 4838 Douglar Ave., Racine, WI 53402-2498. (414) 639-2371.

Mountain Valley Growers, 38325 Pepperweed Rd., Squaw Valley, CA 93675. (209) 338-2775, Fax (209) 338-2775.

Native Seed/SEARCH, 2509 N. Campbell Ave., Tucson, AZ 85719. (602) 327-9123.

The Natural Gardening Co., 217 San Anselmo Ave., San Anselmo, CA 94960. (414) 456-5060, Fax (414) 721-0642.

Nichols Garden Nursery, 1190 North Pacific Highway, Albany, OR 97321-4598. (503) 928-9280, Fax (503) 967-8406.

Owen Nursery, 2300 East Lincoln St., Bloomington, IL 61701. (300) 663-9551.

Park Seed, Cokesbury Rd., Greenwood, SC 29647-0001. (800) 845-3369, Fax (803) 223-6999.

Peace Seeds, 2385 SE Thompson St., Corvallis, OR 97333.

Pinetree Garden Seeds, Route 100, New Gloucester, ME 04260. (207) 926-3400, Fax (207) 926-3886.

Plants of the Southwest, Agua Fria, Route 6 Box 11-A, Santa Fe, NM 87501. (800) 788-7333, Fax (505) 471-2212.

Redwood City Seed Co., PO Box 361, Redwood City, CA 94064. (415) 325-7333.

Richters, Goodwood, Ontario, L0C 1A0, Canada. (416) 640-6677, Fax (416) 640-6641.

Ronniger's Seed Potatoes, Star Route Rd. 73, Movie Springs, ID 83845.

Seeds Blum, Idaho City Stage, Boise, ID 83706. (208) 336-8462.

Seeds of Change, 1364 Rufina Circle #5, Santa Fe, NM 87501-2927. (505) 438) 8080, Fax (505) 438) 7052.

Shepherd's Garden Seeds, 6116 Highway 9, Felton, CA 98018. (408) 335-6910.

Shepherd's Garden Seeds, 30 Irene St., Torrington, CT 06790. (203) 482-3638.

Smith & Hawken, 25 Corte Madera, Mill Valley, CA 94941. (415) 383-2000.

Sonoma Antique Apple Nurse, 4395 Westside Rd., Healdsburg, CA 95448. (707) 433-6420.

Southern Exposure Seed Exchange, PO Box 170-1, Earlysville, VA 22936. (804) 973-4703.

Talavaya, PO Box 707, Santa Cruz Station, Santa Cruz, NM 87567.

Thompson and Morgan, PO Box 1308, Jackson, NJ 08527-0308. (800) 274-7333.

Tomato Growers Supply Co., PO Box 2237, Fort Meyers, FL 33902. (813) 768-1119.

Van Engelem, Inc., Stillbrook Farm, 313 Maple St., Litchfield, CT 06759. (203) 567-8734.

Wayside Gardens, 1 Garden Lane, Hodges, SC 29695-0001. (800) 845-1124.

William Tricker, Inc., 7125 Tanglewood Drive, Independence, OH 44131. (216) 524-3491. Fax (216) 524-6688.

INSECTARY ADDRESSES

Arbico, Inc., PO Box 4247 CRB, Tucson, AZ 85738-1247. (800) 827-2847.

Rincon-Vitova Insectaries, Inc., PO Box 1555, Ventura, CA 93002. (805) 643-5407.

SOCIETIES

American Bat Conservation Society, PO Box 1393, Rockville, MD 20849. (301) 309-6610.

American Community Gardening Association, 325 Walnut St., Philadelphia, PA 19106.

American Horticultural Society, 7931 East Boulevard Drive, Alexandria, VA 22308-1300. (800) 777-7931.

National Audubon Society, PO Box 52529, Boulder, CO 80322. (800) 274-4201.

Xerces Society, 10 SW Ash St., Portland, OR 97204.

Andrews, Jane. *The Stories Mother Nature Told Her Children.* Boston, Massachusetts: Ginn and Company, 1902.

Anna Elizabeth. *Vase of Flowers.* Boston, Massachusetts: G.W. Cottrell, 1851.

Anonymous, J.S. *Friendship's Jewel.* Boston, Massachusetts: J. Buffam, 1851.

Bailey, Liberty Hyde. *Cyclopedia of American Horticulture.* New York, New York: Macmillan and Company Limited, 1900.

———. *Hortus Third.* New York, New York: Macmillan Publishing Company, 1978.

———. *Talks Afield.* Boston, Massachusetts: Houghton, Mifflin, 1885.

———. *The Garden of Gourds.* New York, New York: Macmillan and Company, 1937.

Barnard, D.B. Poem in Nursery Magazine. Boston, Massachusetts: Nursery Publishing, 1880.

Barnhart, Robert. *The American Dictionary of Science.* Boston, Massachusetts: Houghton Mifflin, 1986.

Barrows, Marjorie. *One Hundred Best Poems for Boys and Girls.* Racine, Wisconsin: Whitman Publishing Company, 1930.

Beckett, Kenneth. *Climbing Plants.* Portland, Oregon: Timber Press, 1983.

Bernardino, Minnie. *Passion Fruit, Passion Fruit.* Los Angeles, California: Los Angeles Times, September 17 1992.

Blyton, Enid. *Let's Garden.* London, England: Latimer House Ltd., 1948.

Bone, Gertrude. *The Hidden Orchis.* London, England: The Medici Society, 1928.

Bowman, John. *Happy All Day Through.* Joliet, Illinois: P.F. Volland Company, 1917.

Breck, Joseph. *The Young Florist.* Boston, Massachusetts. Russell, Odiorne and Company, 1833.

Brickell, Christopher and John Elsley. *The American Horticultural Society Encyclopedia of Garden Plants.* New York, New York: Macmillan Publishing, 1989.

Brown, Elizabeth. *Stories of Woods and Fields.* New York, New York: Globe School Book Company, 1902.

Burpee, W. Atlee. *Burpee's 1908 Farm Annual: The Plain Truth About Seeds.* Philadelphia, Pennsylvania: W. Atlee Burpee and Company, 1908.

Bynum, Flora Ann. *Old Salem Garden Guide.* Winston-Salem, North Carolina: Old Salem, Inc., 1979.

Carter, David. *Butterflies and Moths.* New York, New York: Dorling Kindersley, Inc., 1992.

Choate, Ernest A. *The Dictionary of American Bird Names*—Revised Edition. Boston, Massachusetts: The Harvard Common Press, 1985.

Claxton, William J. *Lessons from Nature's Workshop.* New York, New York: Thomas Y. Crowell Company, 1913.

Conant, Grace. *The Children's Year.* Springfield, Massachusetts: Milton Bradley Company, 1915.

Cosy Nook Story Book. Springfield, Massachusetts: McLoughlin Brothers, Inc., 1924.

Cox, E.H.M. *The Gardener's Chapbook.* London, England: Chatto and Windus, 1931.

Cranmer-Byng, L. *A Feast of Lanterns.* London, England. John Murray.

Dana, Mrs. William Starr. *Plants and Their Children.* New York, New York: American Book Company, 1896.

Driscoll, Louise. *Garden Grace.* New York, New York: The Macmillan Company, 1927.

DeGraff, Robert. *The Book of the Toad.* Rochester, Vermont: Park Street Press, 1991.

Edgarton, S.C. *Fables of Flora.* Boston, Massachusetts: Merrill and Heywood, 1844.

Elliot, G.F.S. Scott. *The Romance of Plant Life.* London, England: Seeley, Service and Company, Ltd., 1922.

Emery, Dara. *Seed Propagation of Native California Plants.* Santa Barbara, California: Santa Barbara Botanic Garden, 1988.

Faulkner, Herbert. *The Mysteries of the Flowers.* New York, New York: Frederick A. Stokes Company, 1917.

Field Guide to the Birds of North America. Washington, D.C.: National Geographic Society, 1988.

Field, Henry. *Seeds 1924.* Shenandoah, Iowa: Henry Field, 1924.

Foulke, Elizabeth. *Twilight Stories.* Boston, Massachusetts: Silver-Burdett and Company, 1895.

Gardening for the Many—Being Practical Monthly Directions. London, England: Journal of Horticulture and Cottage Gardener Office, 1865.

Graham, Marguerite. *Fairy Fantasies.* New York, New York: Frederik Lunning, Inc., 1940.

Gutmann, Rudolph. *American Wildflowers.* New York, New York: Hastings House Publisheers, 1946.

Hallock, Grace. *After the Rain.* New York, New York: School Service Cleanliness Institute, 1927.

Holland, John. "Genetic Algorithms". New York, New York: Scientific American, July 1992.

Holmgren, Virginia. *The Way of the Hummingbird.* Santa Barbara, California: Capra Press, 1986.

Hooker, M.D. Worthington. *The Child's Book of Nature.* New York, New York: Harper and Brothers, 1863.

Hooper, Lucy. *The Lady's Book of Flowers and Poetry.* New York, New York: J.D. Rilker, 1847.

Ingpen, Roger. *One Thousand Poems for Children.* Philadelphia, Pennsylvania: Macrae Smith Company, 1920.

Judson, Clara. *Flower Fairies.* New York, New York: Rand McNally and Company, 1915.

Kelly, M.A.B. *Short Stories of Our Shy Neighbors.* New York, New York: American Book Company, 1896.

King, Marie West. *Recipe For A Happy Life.* San Francisco, California: Paul Elder and Company, 1911.

King, Francis. *The Flower Garden Day by Day.* New York, New York: Frederick A. Stokes Company, 1927.

McCurrie, Charles. *Merry Time Songs for Children.* Alameda, California: Alameda Music Company, 1901.

McIlvaine, Charles. *Outdoors and Indoors and Up the Chimney.* Philadelphia, Pennsylvania: The Sunday School Times Company, 1906.

Mitchell, P. Chalmers. *The Pageant of Nature.* London, England: Cassell and Company, Ltd., 1923.

Mitford, Mary. *Our Village.* New York, New York: Dodge Publishing Company, 1911.

Morley, Margaret. *Seed-Babies.* Boston, Massachusetts: Ginn and Company, 1900.

Newman, L. Hugh. *Create A Butterfly Garden.* London, England: John Baker Publishers, Ltd., 1967.

Ogden, Shepherd and Ellen. *The Cook's Garden-Growing and Using the Best-Tasting Vegetable Varieties.* Emmaus, Pennsylvania: Rodale Press, 1989.

Paquin, Samuel Savil. *Garden Fairies.* New York, New York: Moffat, Yard and Company.

Parley, Peter. *A Gift for My Young Friends.* New York, New York: Leavitt and Allen.

Porter, Gene Stratton. *The Keeper of the Bees.* New York, New York: Doubleday, Page and Company, 1925.

Plant Babies. Boston, Massachusetts: Education Publishing Company.

St. Nicholas Songs: 112 Songs by 32 Composers. New York, New York: The Century Company, 1885.

Poulsson, Emilie. *Finger Plays for Nursery and Kindergarten.* D. Lothrop Company, 1893.

Pyle, Robert. *The Audubon Society Handbook for Butterfly Watchers.* New York, New York: Charles Scribner's Sons, 1984.

Quackenbush, Alice. *All In a Garden Fair.* New York, New York: A.T. De La More Company, Inc., 1925.

Quinn, Vernon. *Leaves—Their Place in Life and Legend.* New York, New York: Frederick A. Stokes Company, 1937.

———. *Vegetables in the Garden & Their Legends.* New York, New York: J.B. Lippincott Company, 1942.

Radford, Dollie. *The Young Gardeners Kalendar.* London, England: De La More Press, ND.

Ransom, Jay. *Harper & Row's Complete Field Guide to North American Wildlife.* New York, New York: Harper and Row, 1914.

Richardson, John. *In the Garden of Delight.* Boston, Massachusetts: H.M. Caldwell Company, 1912.

Roderick, Kyle. "The New Naturalism". Los Angeles, California: Los Angeles Times, November 29, 1990.

Rogers, Julia. *Useful Plants Every Child Should Know.* New York, New York: Grosset and Dunlap, 1913.

Rohde, Eleanour. *The Gardener's Week-End Book.* London, England: Seeley Service and Company, Ltd., 1939.

Seddon, Quentin. "Toad in a Hole". London, England: Country Living Magazine (Britain), August 1992.

Sedenko, Jerry. *The Butterfly Garden.* New York, New York: Villard Books, 1991.

Seymour-Jones, Louise. *Who Love a Garden.* The Primavera Press, 1935.

Shackelford, Frederick. *Insect Stories.* San Francisco, California: Harr Wagner Publishing Company, 1940.

Skutch, Alexander. *The Life of the Hummingbird.* New York, New York: Vineyard Books, Inc., 1973.

Taylor, Ida Scott. *My Little Pansy People.* London, England: Raphael Tuck and Sons, 1899.

Taylor, J.E. *The Playtime Naturalist.* New York, New York: D. Appleton and Company, 1889.

Tekulsky, Mathew. *The Butterfly Garden.* Harvard, Massachusetts: The Harvard Common Press, 1954.

Thayer, J. *The Golden Present.* Boston, Massachusetts: G.W. Cottrell and Company, 1853.

Thompson, Blanche Jennings. *More Silver Pennies.* New York, New York: The Macmillan Company, 1938.

———. *Silver Pennies.* New York, New York: The Macmillan Company, 1935.

"Turn On Learning with Bulbs". Burlington, Vermont: Growing Ideas, September 1992.

Untermeyer, Louis. *This Singing World.* New York, New York: Harcourt Brace and Company, 1923.

Wagner, Helga. *Frontiers.* Leipzig: Leipzig Volkszeitung, July 16, 1992.

Woods, Frank. "Children's Gardens Everywhere". New York, New York: *The Garden Magazine*, January 1910.

Index

Slug Eater · Manure Manufacturer